Gabrielle Carey is a writer and author of ten books, including *Moving Among Strangers: Randolph Stow and my family*, which jointly won the 2014 Prime Minister's Award for Non-Fiction and was shortlisted for the National Biography Award, and *Falling Out of Love with Ivan Southall* (2018). Her essay 'Waking Up with James Joyce' was chosen as a Notable Essay in *The Best American Essays* 2019 edition. She teaches creative non-fiction at the University of Technology Sydney. In 2020 Carey was shortlisted for the Hazel Rowley Literary Fellowship for her work on Elizabeth von Arnim.

GABRIELLE CAREY

ONLY HAPPINESS HERE

In search of
Elizabeth von Arnim

First published 2020 by University of Queensland Press
PO Box 6042, St Lucia, Queensland 4067 Australia

uqp.com.au
reception@uqp.uq.edu.au

Cover design by Christabella Designs
Cover photograph by Shutterstock
Typeset in 13.25/16 pt Perpetua MT Std by Post Pre-press Group, Brisbane
Printed in Australia by McPherson's Printing Group

The University of Queensland Press is assisted by
the Australian Government through the Australia
Council, its arts funding and advisory body.

A catalogue record for this book is available from the National Library of Australia

ISBN 978 0 7022 6297 5 (pbk)
ISBN 978 0 7022 6447 4 (epdf)
ISBN 978 0 7022 6448 1 (epub)
ISBN 978 0 7022 6449 8 (kindle)

*Dedicated to Ursula D because
'kindred spirits are so very, very rare'.*

When I discovered Elizabeth von Arnim, I found, for the first time, a writer who wrote about being happy. So much of my reading life – which essentially means so much of my *actual daily* life – had been spent reading miserable literature because, let's face it, most literature *is* miserable. The novel that influenced me most in my early twenties was *Les Misérables*. Then I went on to adore the tragedies of Thomas Hardy, the horrors of Zola, the suffering of Dostoevsky, the pain of Tolstoy and the misfortunes of Henry Handel Richardson. My reading life, which led to my writing life (after which there wasn't much left over), had been misery from cover to cover. Until Elizabeth.

The words 'happy' and 'happiness' occur remarkably frequently in Elizabeth's novels and diaries, contradicting the usual image of 'the writer' as dour, introspective, depressed – the kind of writer I had read, I had known, and I had *been* for most of my life. Elizabeth was the first person to inspire me – even instruct me – on how not to be that kind of writer. Indeed, how not to be that kind of *person*.

As a result, I became something of an Elizabeth von Arnim evangelist, proselytising to everyone I met about this brilliant, Australian-born author who had vanished from literary memory. I felt incensed, on her behalf, that she had been so completely forgotten and soon became possessed, the way biographers do, by the idea of writing a book about her. But just as I was going to put pen to paper, fate intervened. A catastrophic event hit my family that put all my plans on hold, the repercussions of which will be with us forever.

Months later, as we seemed to be beginning to recover, I discovered I had been the victim of a major identity theft that resulted in three loans I had never applied for, from banks I'd never heard of, and a particular kind of chaos that involved a dimension of existence I had spent my life trying to avoid: banks, credit agencies, tax offices, health insurers, mobile phone companies. Countless hours were spent listening to Muzak while I waited to talk to a cyber-security expert about my hacked email account, my ported mobile number, my PayPal password, my stolen Visa card. Then when the police caught the fraudster, completely by accident, the arrest unleashed a series of interviews with detectives, subpoenas, witness statements and a court appearance, where I finally came face-to-face with my imposter and was surprised to find how deeply I hated her. Or was it really my own life I loathed?

By then I had almost completely forgotten what happiness felt like. So depleted was I that I decided to take a year off work, unpaid, with absolutely no idea how I was going to survive. I told myself that I was giving myself time off to recover from the worst year of my life. But my other reason — or I should say my *real* reason — was that taking leave from work would allow me to write. What I didn't realise was how these two projects would become intertwined: reading and writing about Elizabeth would become one of the essential keys to my recovery. If my previous book had taught me about courage and resilience, this one, I hoped, might teach me about happiness.

The first thing that Elizabeth taught me about happiness was that to begin you have to believe. At that stage of my life, I had completely lost faith in the very idea of happiness, let alone the pursuit of it. Whenever anyone used the word I cringed: a trite, meaningless concept, I would reflect privately — a myth that we all continuously subscribed to in the face of a reality that so clearly contradicted our determined denial. Nothing more, in essence, than a collective delusion.

Elizabeth, on the other hand, believed 'that happiness was attainable by all except the unworthy and deluded'. And I found that by ensconcing myself intensely in her novels and her life over a period of a year, my attitude changed from complete cynicism to a gradual openness to the possibility of happiness. She didn't change my mind by way of philosophical argument; it was more like being exposed to an indefinable infection. It was something I *caught*. And although I cannot really explain how, it felt palpably real. I now call it E.E., the Elizabeth Effect.

My quest to learn more about Elizabeth von Arnim was born of an intense admiration of her writing, especially her light touch when satirising the men who were continually trying to thwart her irrepressible spirit. I was also fascinated by her ability to love, laugh and mother five children, while also managing to write a comic novel, on average, every year. Somehow she could do all that and still find time to enjoy picnics and read poetry in the sun. The truth was that I wanted to *be* her: talented, accomplished, funny and also, fairly regularly, rapturously happy.

Elizabeth von Arnim was born in Sydney, in 1866, to an English merchant family. Christened Mary Beauchamp, she was the cousin of the modernist short story writer and poet, Katherine Mansfield (also originally a Beauchamp), and the last person Mansfield wrote to before her untimely death. She was the lover of H.G. Wells, employer of E.M. Forster, a close friend of Bertrand Russell and survived marriages to a brutish German count and a notorious English Earl, all the while producing an enormous body of work. Part satirist, part feminist and part nature writer, she was a passionate gardener and a lover of the outdoors. 'I'm so glad I didn't die on the various occasions I have earnestly wished I might,' she wrote, 'for if I had I would have missed a lot of lovely weather.'

According to the Australian biographer Verna Coleman:

> Elizabeth was a mountain of vanity and had the will power to fight for what she thought her due. A powerful personality – fearless, determined, able, clever. She created a persona that took her to comparative heights for an Australian-born intruder of no class standing. Talented, musical, petite and pretty – definitely a girl from far away, even a girl from nowhere. This was the girl that was to become a tough-minded Prussian aristocrat and a dryly comic observer of European and English life.

Of all the many literary figures I have admired over the years, if there was one writer I could go back in time and spend a day with it would be Elizabeth. In part for her intellect and wit, but mostly because I'm absolutely certain she would be great fun. That is, if she thought my company worthwhile. According to Australian-born writer Deborah Kellaway:

> If she thought you stupid, or hidebound, she would make you shrivel under her contempt and impatience. But if you amused her she would be, in return, like a glass of champagne: sparkling, dry, lifting the present moment until it blotted out all humdrum anxieties and fears for the past and future, and leaving a sense of flatness behind her when she went away.

Which is how I feel whenever I put down one of her novels – I miss her sparkling presence. But I only need go back to one of the books I haven't read for a while and pick up any page and she will always make me laugh or marvel or feel grateful – as though she were letting me in on some essential secret about how to live, but without ever spelling it out. I simply feel uplifted by her spirit, or what others might call her *joie de vivre*.

Over the door of Elizabeth's expansive Swiss chalet, where she spent many summers entertaining authors, critics, philosophers and intellectuals, were inscribed the words: 'Only Happiness Here.' She had little sympathy for misery gutses:

> Bother the gloomy. They are an ungrateful set. If they can they will turn the whole world sour, and sap up all the happiness ... without giving out any shining in return. I am all for sun, and heat, and colour, and scent – for all things radiant and positive.

She was perhaps, unknowingly, one of the earliest proponents of positive psychology. Even in the year before she died, as an old woman – when her fame and wealth and celebrity and health were fading – she still noted in her diary: 'I think I've so got into the habit of being happy inside and quite secretly ...'

Maybe, I thought, instead of paying for monthly therapy sessions, consuming expensive antidepressants and reading books like *Happiness by Design*, *The Happiness Plan* and *The Happiness Trap* I could just follow Elizabeth's lead. But how did she do it?

Perhaps the way to begin was to re-read every one of her twenty-one books. The first time round I had read them for enjoyment and entertainment – because they made me laugh. This time I would read them with a question: what did Elizabeth von Arnim understand about happiness that no other writer I've ever come across did? And is it something I too might be able to learn?

My re-established faith in happiness didn't happen in a lightning strike or any kind of Kierkegaardian leap. It began slowly, in a sense, without me even being aware of it. The fact that I had taken a year out of my paid job to devote to Elizabeth was the first sign. Then, when I was offered a fellowship just a few months into my self-imposed unemployment, I took it as an affirmation and my tentative faith took wings.

My research into Elizabeth's life led me to London during the English summer heatwave of 2018. At the airport I ticked 'Conference' on my arrival card as the reason for visiting – the following week I was due to give a paper at the International Centre for Victorian Women Writers at Canterbury Christ Church University. This was my ostensible motive for flying halfway around the world as well as my justification for the expense. After all, I could hardly declare my real intention: 'Searching for Elizabeth von Arnim's secret to happiness.'

On arrival, my first destination was St Paul's Cathedral.

During Elizabeth's almost manically restless life, she used
St Paul's as her centre of gravity, a kind of grounding place she
always came back to in times of grief, and also in times of
gratitude. She was not religious in a conventional sense and
loathed the hypocrisy of the church hierarchy, but she adored
churches and several of her many tours of England were
arranged specifically around cathedrals. When in London,
St Paul's was a refuge she frequently used while in the throes
of making major decisions or recovering from relationship
woes, and she once spent an entire day there 'meditating'.

Outside the cathedral I admired a bronze bust of John
Donne, about whom I remembered writing an essay while at
East Sydney Technical College in the late 1970s. This was
during my half-hearted attempt to complete my Higher School
Certificate after walking out of secondary school at fifteen.
While contemplating the Donne memorial, an image of my
long-suffering English lecturer resurfaced in my consciousness
for the first time in forty years – an earnest, bearded enthusiast
doing his best to introduce a motley bunch of drop-outs to
seventeenth century religious poetry. I still own my copy of
the set text, *The Metaphysical Poets*, the pages of which bear
witness to the only evidence of genuine study from that year
of 1979. Around Donne's 'The Extasie', the margins are
crammed with neat Biro notations in a childish print. My
teenage commentary includes a statement that the poem is
about 'the Relationship of Soul and Sense' and is 'the poet's
philosophical discussion with himself about real love' – clearly
comments directly taken down from my lecturer. Later, having

studied the poem at length, I decided it was just a long waffly attempt by Donne to open the legs of his latest object of desire, and replaced the title with my own re-write: 'Ode to a Tightarse by Professional Sweet-talker' – based on the lingo of the Sutherland Shire; 'tightarse' meaning any girl who didn't immediately submit to masculine gropings. For that reason, I had retained an impression of John Donne as part-poet and part-sleaze. I was surprised, therefore, to learn from the plaque beneath the bust that he had once been Dean of St Paul's.

Inside the cathedral I found a front-row seat for the service of Holy Communion, which was celebrating the Feast of Mary Magdalene. The sermon was refreshingly intelligent, reflecting on how the original version of the gospels was a collection of messy stories about messy lives such as Magdalene's – and that over the years, in order to make the characters more respectable, the stories had been tidied up. It was odd to think that even the gospels were once rough drafts with loose ends, and how editors had managed to make them more presentable and palatable to reading audiences. These days, of course, the drafts would be subject to marketability questions during acquisitions meetings prior to publication: *But how much social media presence do these authors have?*

For the next sweltering week, every morning I caught the crowded bus to the British Library and admired the stoicism of the English commuters as they sat and sweated quietly without complaint. My days were spent in the tepid reading rooms leafing through correspondence between

Elizabeth and her publishers, searching for clues, for telling details, for that thing that all researchers are always looking for – a story, an admission, a secret that no one else has noticed, that has remained hidden in the archives for over a century, only to be discovered by an Australian interloper. But I found nothing particularly new or startling. Perhaps, as I'd always suspected, I wasn't a scholar at all, and nothing more than a highly educated gossip.

At this point it became clear to me that my intention was not to pen a conventional biography – three of which already existed – but to share my love of Elizabeth and her works with readers outside of the scholarly world. She wasn't my 'subject' or my 'research project'; she was more like a very special friend that I was aching to introduce to everyone I knew. And even to people I didn't know.

The day that Elizabeth – then Mary Annette Beauchamp – was born, 31 August, is the day before Wattle Day, celebrating the start of the Australian spring, and it is likely the fragrant blooms were on show along the sandy bushland shores of the harbour on the morning that Elizabeth came into the world.

Louey Beauchamp's sixth and final labour was a difficult one and from then on she withdrew all wifely duties of a sexual nature and retreated to the sofa, claiming a headache. In response, her husband, Henry, stayed out, took up a mistress and 'was seen in the company of the rather more boisterous ladies of the town'. Elizabeth commented later that she believed her father 'wasn't a man who ought ever to have had any children except grown-up ones'.

The Beauchamps were notoriously restless and Henry travelled a lot, often months at a time, perhaps in part as a way of avoiding his offspring. As a child, Elizabeth noticed the marked difference in the atmosphere at home when her father was absent.

> Queer how sprightly life became, how roomy, with what wide margins, when my father, in those years, wasn't there. For my part, instead of taut I became happy-go-lucky; instead of minding my p's and q's and watching my steps, I ceased to mind or watch anything.

During her father's lengthy absences, there was also a great change in Elizabeth's mother. She no longer restricted herself to the couch but instead became 'independent and tremendously gay'. This set the pattern for Elizabeth's inescapable belief 'that feminine talents for enjoyment were more than likely to be suppressed by the egotism of men'.

Elizabeth's father, Henry Herron Beauchamp, settled in Sydney in 1850 at the age of twenty-five. His career as a merchant was helped by his marriage to Louey Lassetter, the sister of a prominent Sydney merchant, Frederic Lassetter, who had made his fortune supplying goods to migrants and miners, and then through establishing Lassetter's Stores, a thriving retail emporium in George Street. When Fred Lassetter decided to take his family back to England in 1869, he encouraged his brother-in-law to do the same and, by way of persuasion, sent him a draft for 200 pounds. The Beauchamps auctioned off their household effects, including 'brilliant-tone pianofortes', 'richly cut glass', 'first-class Electro-plate' and 'every requisite for a gentleman's family'. With all their chattels disposed of, the family boarded the sailing ship *La Hogue* on 11 January 1870. Elizabeth was three years old.

The Beauchamp family arrived in London in April 1870. Elizabeth's first home in England was in Hampstead, barely a mile from the location of her cousin Katherine Mansfield's later home, between 1918 and 1920, nicknamed 'The Elephant'.

Little May, as Elizabeth was known to her family, was the youngest of a big brood, as well as being a girl after four boys who were 'as thick as thieves', and this meant she had to compete hard for attention. Teased mercilessly by her elder brothers, she claimed that she always felt an 'apartness in the family'.

'However arresting what she had to say, no one wanted to listen,' writes her daughter. 'She therefore committed it to paper.'

Withdrawing into privacy provided a space that allowed her to develop a toughness as well as an astute critical eye, particularly regarding male behaviour. By the time she was an adult, thanks to her childhood experience, Elizabeth had developed into such a virtuosic tease that her barbs often bordered on malice, a side to her that E.M. Forster would later describe as 'cruel and steely' and on one occasion reduced the young Hugh Walpole to tears. It was this talent, I believe, that allowed her to develop her gift for satire, which was similarly steely but always funny.

By her early teens, Elizabeth's speech, according to biographer Karen Usborne, 'had nearly lost its Australian twang' but another researcher, Verna Coleman, believes she maintained an accent all her life.

'The one remnant of May's childhood idyll in her grown-up life was a curious accent. To cover this she murmured vaguely to H.G. Wells about Irish connections.' Wells believed her and wrote in his autobiography: 'She was Irish, with an Irish passion for absurdity and laughter.'

Others, such as E.M. Forster, called Elizabeth's voice 'grating'. He at least knew her origins, and in his 1959 article about his memories of Elizabeth, considered her birthplace of peculiar interest, even putting an exclamation mark after 'Australia!'. The novelist Frank Swinnerton described her as 'lazy-voiced'. Another acquaintance thought of her as crooning aloud rather than talking and described her 'u' as French. When she arrived late for lunch, he portrayed her speech as follows: 'Du forgive me, will yiu?'

Whether it was an Australian drawl or a French croon, Elizabeth clearly had a very distinct voice, something she possibly worked on, maybe even in an attempt to hide her colonial origins.

Following her education at Queen's College, Elizabeth attended the Royal College of Music and learnt to play Bach fugues on the organ of St George's Chapel, under the tutelage of Sir Walter Parratt, organist at Windsor Castle. Her intention was to sit the university entrance examination for Cambridge but she became ill and missed the exam. 'She was now eighteen, and was expected to stay at home and be a comfort to her parents,' her daughter Liebet wrote in a biography of her mother, *Elizabeth of the German Garden*, 'until, in due time, she became a comfort to a husband.'

The family made no effort at the expensive business of the youngest daughter's 'coming out', according to Elizabeth's elder sister, Charlotte, because they assumed that 'poor lonely little May' would never make a brilliant match. In her parents' eyes, Elizabeth's cleverness and sharp tongue were attributes that no potential suitor would find appealing. Elizabeth added to these undesirable qualities by refusing to make herself attractive to potential husbands, 'and began to affect a simplicity of dress and hair arrangement that was severe'. She was already beginning to display signs of an independent, feminist spirit she would go on to develop and even talked about going out to work as a street-sweeper (as does the frustrated heroine of her first full-length novel *The Benefactress*). Rebellious and determined, the youngest Beauchamp appeared to prefer playing music, reading and gardening to the idea of finding a wealthy husband.

Increasingly irritated by her daughter's wilful refusal to take marriage seriously, Elizabeth's mother became genuinely concerned, afraid she might become a 'frost-bitten virgin'.

Twenty-three was considered to be an advancing age and so a tour of Europe was embarked upon with the specific purpose of marrying off the only Beauchamp girl who remained unattached.

Before leaving England, the Beauchamp family obtained a letter of introduction from Sir George Grove and while in Rome it was arranged that their youngest daughter would give two recitals on the organ of the American Episcopal Church. One of the author's many talents was a remarkable musical ability, including perfect pitch. Like Henry Handel Richardson, another 'girl from far away', May Beauchamp was a gifted keyboardist and composer. If being a professional musician had been possible for a woman in those days, she may well have chosen that path, but her main instrument was the organ and women at that time were not permitted to be employed as organists in churches.

Among those invited to hear her was the Count Henning August von Arnim-Schlagenthin, also a talented pianist, and a student of Liszt. It was upon hearing the young Miss Beauchamp play Bach fugues that her future husband, fifteen years her senior, fell in love. Three days later he proposed, according to Elizabeth's memoir, while sight-seeing in Florence.

He followed me, panting a little, for, like other good Germans in those days who had ceased to be young, he wasn't thin, up the steps of the Duomo in Florence, on the top of which he was taking me in order to show me the view, he was addressing me thus: 'All girls like love. It is very agreeable. You will like it too. You shall marry me and see.'

And having arrived at the top he immediately and voluminously embraced me. I remember I struggled. Being embraced was entirely new to me, and I didn't at all like it. That he should explain, too, when at last he let me go, that this was but a beginning, alarmed rather than reassured me.

The scene was directly transferred to <u>the novel many believe to be her best,</u> (*The Pastor's Wife.*) In that book the suitor, Pastor Dremmel, also pants as he struggles up to the peak of Rigi in Lucerne with the purpose of proposing, and afterwards his intended, Ingeborg, is similarly uncomfortable in his uninvited embrace.

'"Oh, but I can't – I won't – oh, stop – oh, stop – it's a mistake –" she tried to get out in gasps.'

Being 'clutched' by Dremmel was something the character Ingeborg 'profoundly disliked' and she 'greatly suspected, now she came to a calm consideration of it, that that was what was the matter with marriage: it was a series of clutchings'.

As the Count pursued Elizabeth all around Europe her status in the family was instantly elevated from 'poor sad little May' to the girl who was possibly going to make the most illustrious match of the entire extended Beauchamp family. As she records in her memoir: 'I also was delighted by my sudden importance in the family. Up to then I had been nobody and suddenly to be somebody, or indeed for a time everybody,

I must say was very pleasant.' Elizabeth clearly revelled in the feeling of being adored, a feeling she pursued and often achieved, throughout the rest of her life.

Following their engagement, the Count suggested that the Beauchamp family travel to Bayreuth for the Wagner festival, an idea that the musically passionate Elizabeth found immediately seductive. There they attended *Die Meistersinger von Nürnberg*, *Tristan und Isolde* and *Parsifal* at Festival House, which had been constructed according to Wagner's design. She was introduced to the Wagner family as well as the von Arnim relatives and mixed with German high society, giving her the opportunity to practise being a Prussian Countess. Elizabeth's mother wrote a letter to her half-sister Jessie, reporting the highlights of their stay in Bayreuth:

> Last night we went to a grand reception at Madame Wagner's. I never was in such a lovely house or met so many distinguished people. Dear little May looking very charming in a lovely evening dress Chaddie gave her, cream, and the Count gave her a bunch of pink roses which she wore. He was devoted all evening.

Despite Elizabeth's rise in status within the family, she was still wearing hand-me-downs from her big sister, Charlotte. But perhaps what is most pertinent about this letter is the comment that the Count was 'devoted all evening', addressing his fiancée by the pet name of 'Dollie', and leading Elizabeth to trust that these devotions would continue after their marriage.

Whereas previously Henry and Louey Beauchamp had hoped for a wealthy husband for their youngest daughter, they now worried that the Count was perhaps *too* noble and became concerned about how their daughter would adapt to German aristocracy, known as *Junker* society.

'I think as I did from the very first that it would be better for her if she married in her own set,' Louey expressed her private reservations to a letter home.

Notwithstanding her parents' doubts, Elizabeth was now in the power of her fiancé, who was convinced that she was the perfect replacement for his first wife who had recently died in labour, along with their infant. Henning announced that the future Countess would have to be able to speak German, not just for social occasions but for managing their household and supervising the servants. To that purpose, he arranged for Elizabeth and her mother to be installed in a pension in Dresden, where German lessons would be conducted daily. Up until then, Elizabeth and her intended had spoken in French because Henning spoke limited English, and presumably read even less. (This was possibly an advantage later when Elizabeth was writing her novels, which included scenes that featured her husband in a comically unflattering light.)

Daily German lessons were conducted in Dresden while Elizabeth's mother stayed on as chaperone and her father returned to England. But Louey's letters to her husband grew despondent; Dresden had none of the entertainment or high life of Bayreuth and Henry was eventually duty-bound to collect his wife and daughter and take them back to London.

As the engagement extended from weeks to months, Elizabeth's parents began to worry about the lack of a date for the wedding. In addition, although Henning had a title and property, his financial situation was uncertain, having inherited heavy debts from his father. Indeed, his career as an army officer, unsuccessful banker and then experimental farmer, were anything but illustrious. Henry Beauchamp eventually made it clear to the wooing Count that he needed to sort out his finances before any further courting was pursued. When this had no effect and the date for the marriage was still unset, Henry lost patience and insisted that Elizabeth break off the engagement.

At this point, the biographies disagree about what happened next. The general facts are as follows: Elizabeth arranged to take a holiday at a cottage in Goring, only 'scantily chaperoned' by a German maid, while it was agreed that the Count would stay nearby. It was here, in the holiday cottage by the river Thames, according to one version, that Elizabeth lost her virginity. The more recent biography, however, argues that Elizabeth could not have lost her virginity at this time – based on the fact that she did not fall pregnant (her fertility was so robust that she later joked that her husband could impregnate her simply by blowing his nose in the same room as her). Whatever happened, it was understood by her parents that a liaison of some intimacy had occurred and this meant Elizabeth's reputation was at risk and a date for the marriage had to be fixed.

Despite such an intense and often glamorous courtship, it appears Elizabeth still retained some instinctive misgivings about marriage. Her mother wrote home: 'May is so funny about getting married. She says she absolutely refuses to be present at her own wedding as she could not endure the agony of it.'

In her memoir written late in life, Elizabeth reflected on the transition from childhood to marriage, implying it happened almost without her active participation: 'There was a gap ... which I filled by growing up and marrying – or rather being married, because I don't think I had much to do with it ... The man who married me was a German.'

Similarly, in *The Pastor's Wife*, the passive heroine allows herself to be married to her German suitor without ever voicing consent. 'Ingeborg in her bewilderment let these things happen to her.'

How well I understood this experience of letting things happen. All my life I had let things happen to me, often without my consent. I let things happen to me as a young surfie chick in Cronulla – when at least immaturity might be offered as an excuse. But then, as a grown woman I continued to let things happen to me. Indeed, right up until my fifties I just let things happen.

Now, in my sixties, I have belatedly asked myself why. The easy answer is that I was being a stereotypical people-pleasing female seeking male attention and approval. But there was more to it than that. Being of an essentially religious temperament – an aspect of myself I have often felt uncomfortable about – I've always believed that being open to chance is a way of being receptive to grace. For as long as I can remember, I've been deeply committed to chance and serendipity, and suspicious of the idea of self-determination. I was always attracted, for example, to the image of the Irish monks getting into their *curraghs* and letting the wind blow them towards a destination chosen by providence. I also frequently liked to quote the Jewish saying: 'If you want to make God laugh, tell Him your plans.' In other words, there was some part of me that deeply believed in the cloud of unknowing, especially not knowing who I was or what I wanted or what was best for me. So why not let life happen? Why not say yes to every experience, however risky? Wasn't 'yes' the last and ultimate word in one of my favourite books, James Joyce's *Ulysses*? Isn't a 'yes' also a yes to life?

I am a slow learner so it wasn't until very late in my development that I realised how dangerous this determined openness to chance and risk really is, particularly when it comes to relationships with men. As Elizabeth's husband says in her first semi-autobiographical diary–novel, 'Creatures who habitually say *yes* to everything a man proposes, when no one can oblige them to say it, and when it is so often fatal, are plainly not responsible beings.'

Now that I can look back on my past relationships with a measure of serenity, I realise that the Count was right: I was plainly not a responsible being. Indeed, I was positively giddy.

It is only now, at this very late stage of life, when I have finally arrived at a state of semi-sobriety, that I can take solace in the fact that the supremely intelligent and insightful Elizabeth also continued, until well into her middle age, to 'let things happen to her'. She loved men and men loved her, so there was much that was let happen. And though some of it was tragic and some of it was just stupid, I don't think she had many regrets. After all, the words 'happen', 'happenstance' and 'happy' are etymologically connected for a reason.

Elizabeth and Henning entered into wedlock on 6 February 1891 at the Church of St Stephen in Kensington. In that moment the girl from colonial Kirribilli became a Prussian Countess. The newlyweds then travelled to Paris for a brief honeymoon, which was apparently profoundly disillusioning.

In her novels Elizabeth was to write often about the disappointment that follows the heady falling-in-love stage of a relationship. The novel that seems to be most closely modelled on her own marriage, *The Pastor's Wife*, has the heroine reflecting hopefully during the aftermath of her wedding that, 'Perhaps this will grow on me'. But by the fourth day she has decided 'that probably she had no gift for honeymoons'.

'Whatever happened,' writes von Arnim's most recent biographer, Jennifer Walker — who refers to the author by her christened, rather than her assumed name — 'it seems that

Mary, with her passionate nature, was left with longings that were as yet unfulfilled.'

My impression is that Henning's transformation from an utterly devoted lover to a proprietorial husband was as sudden and profound as it was incomprehensible. Later, Elizabeth was to write in her memoir:

> Who indulges more recklessly in glowing exaggerations than the lover who hopes, and has not yet obtained? He will, like the nightingale, sing with unceasing modulations, display all his talent, untiringly repeat his sweetest notes, until he has what he wants, when his song, like the nightingale's, immediately ceases, never again to be heard.

Karen Usborne, von Arnim's 1986 biographer, comments that: 'Now that they were married Henning's attitude towards Elizabeth changed ... She had become his property and a German. German wives were not supposed to think or act for themselves and were entirely under the domination of their husbands.' (The fact that becoming a German meant losing her British nationality would have serious consequences for Elizabeth later.)

Upon arrival in Berlin, Elizabeth was further disappointed because Henning's luxurious house had been sold and they were to live in an apartment. There was no outdoor space or garden for her to retreat to. Her one consolation, on arriving in her new home, was being greeted by Cornelia, the dog that had belonged to Henning's first wife. Elizabeth later recalled that the dachshund 'whimpered round me, in delighted recognition that here at last was a playmate'. Elizabeth couldn't resist picking up her newfound friend and giving the dog a kiss, upon which Henning immediately admonished her: 'Do not kiss the dog. No dog should be kissed. I have provided you, for kissing purposes, with myself.'

We can perhaps assume that Henning, by this point, was no longer addressing her in French.

For the next five years Elizabeth undertook her arduous transformation from English middle-class to upper-class *Junker* society, something similar to a commoner entering the Royal Family. Elizabeth's German was competent but initially she retained an accent and was still seen as a foreigner. As well as the traditional womanly responsibilities, she was also in charge of an entourage of servants and the sudden leap from girlish games to wifely duties was shockingly abrupt. Only six months previously her governess had been commanding her to 'go upstairs at once and wash' as though she were a child. Elizabeth reflected in her memoir:

> How could a person, used to that sort of thing, all at once start looking lofty, and issuing decrees to people manifestly twice her age? It wasn't really to be expected of me, whose whole life till then had been spent receiving orders, that I should suddenly turn

round and give them. These things can't be done in such a hurry. One has to get one's breath.

In Berlin the dachshund Cornelia was to become Elizabeth's closest companion – one of the fourteen dogs she owned and loved throughout her lifetime.

> That first year of marriage, Cornelia and I were everything to each other. Alone all day from directly after breakfast till evening, because my husband went off early to inspect his remoter farms and didn't come back till dark, if I wished to talk I had to talk to Cornelia.

Lonely and alienated, this was the period in which Elizabeth was forced to develop what she later referred to as her 'stout-heartedness', what we would now call resilience. Cut off from her family and English culture, she made a habit of fleeing the flat to take Cornelia for walks in the neighbouring forests. She also took up bicycling in the mornings so that when most *hausfrauen* were in the kitchen organising their households, Elizabeth was busily pedalling away from the burden of domestic responsibilities. Cycling and romping in the forests, however, were soon curtailed when she discovered she was pregnant.

As far as her husband was concerned, producing an heir was the main purpose of a wife. (His previous wife had died in the attempt.) German wives were intended not only to reproduce but to thoroughly enjoy the process.

In *The Pastor's Wife*, the protagonist, Ingeborg, is taken aback when she realises that her husband expects his wife to spend the rest of her life producing children instead of assisting him to write letters and sermons, as she has done previously for her bishop father, tasks that had given her some measure of satisfaction and achievement.

> 'Children?' said Ingeborg.
> She dropped her arms and looked at him. She had not thought of children.
> 'Then, indeed, my little wife will not wish to write letters or compose sermons.'
> 'Why?' said Ingeborg.
> 'Because you will be a happy mother.'
> 'But don't happy mothers—'
> 'You will be entirely engaged in adoring your children. Nothing else in the world will interest you.'
> Ingeborg stood looking at him with a surprised face. 'Oh?' she said. 'Shall I?'

When Ingeborg falls pregnant she feels increasingly depressed by the changes in her body:

> She had little spirit. She was more tired every day ... She felt humiliated, ashamed of her awkward, distorted body. It was as though she had suddenly grown old ... She would have been transfigured by her shining thoughts if anything could have transfigured

her. But her thoughts, however bright, could not pierce through the sad body. Her outlines were not the outlines for heroic attitudes. She not only had a double chin, she seemed to be doubled over.

Elizabeth was clearly not comfortable with the physical and emotional burden of pregnancy. The young Countess took solace in books, and in particular in the work of her famous forebear by marriage, the wildly unconventional writer and confidante of Beethoven and Goethe, Bettina Brentano. Of pregnancy, Brentano had written: 'A woman is very good and very enlightened who does not hate the man who put her in this state.'

If Elizabeth did not enjoy the physical impediments of her first pregnancy, neither did she look forward to labour. She was aware of advances in medicine to assist with pain relief and raised the subject with her husband. His response, we can assume, was similar to the response that Ingeborg receives from her husband in *The Pastor's Wife*.

> 'Chloroform?' he repeated ... 'What for?'
> 'So I don't know about anything ...'
> 'But this is cowardice,' he said.
> 'I'd like some chloroform,' said Ingeborg.
> 'It's against nature,' said Herr Dremmel.

When Elizabeth asked Henning if she could return to London for the birth – where her brother, a well-respected obstetrician could assist – the idea was immediately dismissed. 'It was considered unpatriotic for a young *Gräfin* to want to have a child anywhere but on German soil.'

Elizabeth's first labour was excruciating and lasted for almost two days. Accompanied only by an utterly unsympathetic doctor, she believed she was going to die. We can presume, once again, that her feelings are reflected in Ingeborg's description of labour: 'She was nothing but a squirming thing without a soul ... without anything but a terrible, awful body.'

According to one biographer 'the experience was shattering' and Elizabeth was left traumatised. Afterwards the new mother was unwell and unable to breastfeed. She believed she was never going to be the same again and became 'suspicious of life'. Later she was to recall that she never quite regained her former strength and vigour. She also suffered from what we would now call post-natal depression, her father referring to an illness directly after the birth that was 'awkward' but without specifying any symptoms.

In addition, her husband was disappointed because she had given birth to a girl, instead of the expected heir, although simultaneously relieved that Elizabeth had survived the ordeal. Henning wrote to Elizabeth's family 'for the first time, perhaps, in English' to announce the birth. Eva Sophie Louise Anna Felicitas, later known simply as Evi, had arrived.

Henning remained determined to procure a son and despite his wife's delicate physical and emotional condition, five months later, to her distress, Elizabeth realised she was pregnant again. (Many years later she managed to joke about these first two children who 'were so close together they were almost twins'.) Her second labour was also long and again undergone without the help of chloroform. 'It was considered to be unnatural and unpatriotic to bear German children without suffering'. But at least this time she was able to breastfeed. Christened Elizabeth but known as 'Liebet', Elizabeth's second daughter was the only one of her five children who was suckled by her mother and also the child with whom she remained closest all her life. Under the pen name Leslie de Charms, Liebet was also Elizabeth's first biographer.

When the mother of two discovered, within months, that she was pregnant for a third time, she became 'bitterly rebellious' and insisted that this time she would go to England for the birth. Her third daughter, Beatrix, was born in London in 1894 'to everyone's huge disappointment' and no doubt Elizabeth felt like a failure for giving birth to another girl when a boy was so longed for. 'Poor little May,' her father wrote in his journal, 'is smothered in babies.'

In order to accommodate her growing brood, in 1896 Elizabeth found a larger apartment in Berlin. 'She and Henning were living almost entirely separate lives by then,' writes Usborne, 'she with the children and he inspecting his estates.' In her new abode, Elizabeth ran the household, played with her children and went to the opera in the evening.

As well as a 'stout-hearted' temperament, Elizabeth was highly disciplined and strong in her resolve about leading an independent life, as far as was possible under such constrictive circumstances. Refusing Henning the very thing he wanted most would have taken enormous courage but according to Liebet, her mother:

> developed a firmness, a reasoned defence of the conclusions she had arrived at with regard to this subject and triumphed, for the time being, over the very different views held by her husband, generation and adopted country.

In other words, Elizabeth refused to have sex with her husband. In response, Henning took a mistress and the stormy scenes that would come to characterise their marriage ensued. Later she was to record: 'Those five years were spent in a flat in a town, and during their whole interminable length I was perfectly miserable.' And yet despite the misery, or perhaps as a way of rising above it, she found enough strength to resolve, for the first time, 'to spend more time on writing stories and none at all on further reproduction'.

If there is one thing that Elizabeth von Arnim excels at in her novels, it's the accurate and often darkly hilarious depiction of marriage. One English reviewer even believed that her books had the power to put women off marrying altogether. From my point of view, Elizabeth was the first writer, after a lifetime of reading, who really told the truth about marriage. Some might argue that I come from a jaundiced viewpoint, given my series of unrewarding relationships and my failure as a wife. Having tried four times, I have come to the conclusion that I too have 'no gift for the married state'. So it is consoling for a serial bolter like myself to know that even the wildly successful and popular Elizabeth also found marriage unmanageable; that she too found the heady falling-in-love stage irresistible and the domestic-drudgery stage that followed unbearable; that she too preferred lovers to husbands.

If this seems like an outlandish attitude now, how much more outrageous it must have been in the early 1900s when Elizabeth was publishing her novels. And how odd, I can't help thinking, that it was a nineteenth century writer who spoke truth to my twentieth century experience of wedlock, and helped me to feel less alone and – ever so slightly – less of a failure. Because whatever small measure of success I might enjoy professionally, it never quite compensates for my failure at being a wife.

The idea that the family home is a happy place and that domestic happiness is the woman's responsibility was an ideal that Elizabeth admired and believed in, but also deeply doubted. Her most enduring novel, *The Enchanted April*, opens with two English housewives meeting in a women's club on a dismal London morning. While the rain hammers down outside, the sweetly submissive, church-going Mrs Arbuthnot attempts to defend the ideal of happy domesticity by quoting from a hymn about heaven and hearth being kindred points, assuring the restless Mrs Wilkins, who is plotting an escape to Italy, that 'Heaven is in our home'. Mrs Wilkins' response is blunt:

'It isn't.'
Mrs. Arbuthnot was taken aback. Then she said gently, 'Oh but it is. It is there if we choose, if we make it.'
'I do choose, and I do make it, and it isn't,' said Mrs. Wilkins.
Then Mrs Arbuthnot was silent, for she too sometimes had doubts about homes.

In an unpublished essay on women, Elizabeth wrote in an unusually sober, almost didactic manner about the clear division between those women who easily meet the requirements of marriage and the concomitant duties of maintaining a happy home, and those who don't:

The thinking required of a wife and mother is not hard, it is quite easy: for all that is needed is that she should ask herself at intervals, 'Now what shall I do next to make them happy?' And given what makes people happy in homes are things like bright fires, and crisp toast, and plenty of hot water, and good temper, and a steady principle of strict non-inquiry, she has only to go and put another log on, or order fresh toast, or smile away a frown, or refrain from a question, and the thing is done ... It seems quite fair: she loves him, and he feeds her; she makes him comfortable, and he clothes her; she gives him children, and he keeps her warm.

However, she continues:

> ... not all women are gifted with the tender passivity, the brooding placidity which makes the perfect wife and mother. Some of them prefer personal freedom to any amount of provided bread and better. Some of them think that the first essential to happiness is freedom ... they suspect that no one is really free who eats somebody else's bread and butter, and feel that the minute a woman does that she is entangled in a situation in which permissions have to be asked and injunctions obeyed ...

Upon reading this essay I finally felt I had uncovered a clue about Elizabeth's happiness philosophy. Here was what I had been looking for: 'the first essential to happiness is freedom'. She was unequivocal. I picked up my silver-plated Caran d'Ache fountain pen, the one I use exclusively for special occasions, and wrote:

Principles of Happiness According to Elizabeth von Arnim

Happiness Principle Number One:
Freedom

Elizabeth's first diary entry for the year of 1896, the year she turned thirty, notes: 'Wrote FW a.m.', an acronym for a work in progress that very probably developed into *The Pastor's Wife*. Given that Henning considered himself an agriculturalist and spent his days inspecting his farms, perhaps 'FW' stood for *Farmer's Wife*.

It is possible that during this period Elizabeth was keeping her writing a secret. Maybe because it was the only activity that truly belonged to her – an indulgence – but perhaps also because of the general attitude at that time towards women writers, reflected in a comment by a character in von Arnim's first book: 'But a girl who writes books – why, it isn't respectable!'

In March of 1896, presumably motivated by a longing to escape Berlin, Elizabeth accompanied her husband to one of his properties in Pomerania known as Nassenheide, an estate of 8000 acres. There she found a seventeenth century *schloss*, the German version of a château, which had once been a convent, but had lain empty for twenty-five years.

She wrote later that she loved 'the beautiful purity of the house, empty of servants and upholstery'. Immediately Elizabeth embarked on restoring the sprawling mansion, arranging for workmen to whitewash the interior walls, a practice that was usually reserved for pigsties. She cleaned out an upstairs bedroom and persuaded her husband to allow her to live there, on the pretext of supervising the painters and decorators, while Henning returned to Berlin where the children had been left in the care of a nanny.

The moment that her husband left, Elizabeth's happiness principle number one came into effect. Rather than being housebound and focused on domestic duties, she mostly ignored the renovations going on indoors and spent her days in the garden. Instead of the heavy German meals that she loathed (so well satirised in Katherine Mansfield's story 'Germans at Meat'), Elizabeth now lived on picnics of brown bread and salad. Here she found her longed-for privacy and could indulge in her almost religious communing with nature. The book that she had begun to write in Berlin, referred to as 'FW', was dropped and she turned instead to drafting what was to become her first best-seller *Elizabeth and her German Garden*, in which she recorded the joy of her long-awaited freedom:

> During those six weeks I lived in a world of dandelions and delights ... the acacias all blossomed too, and four great clumps of pale, silvery-pink peonies flowered under the south windows, I felt absolutely happy, and blest, and thankful and grateful, that I really cannot describe it. My days seemed to melt away in a dream of pink and purple peace.

Elizabeth and her German Garden is now referred to as a novel but it is written in diary form and gives the impression of being a slightly fictionalised version of Elizabeth's life at the time. How truly autobiographical the book is remains debatable. Throughout her 2013 biography of von Arnim,

Jennifer Walker refers to the writer by her christened name of Mary and 'Elizabeth' only in inverted commas. She believes the persona of Elizabeth is pure illusion and warns readers that we cannot take her literally. 'The mask of Elizabeth is carefully and skilfully constructed. But Elizabeth is not Mary.'

However, according to novelist, Frank Swinnerton, who knew Elizabeth personally, the voice behind *Elizabeth and her German Garden* was no alter ego: 'What she seemed to be in *Elizabeth and her German Garden* ... she was in reality.' The narrator of the diary–novel *was* identical to Elizabeth herself.

🌿

After five years of living in Berlin and 'somewhat mutinously' bearing three children in three years, Elizabeth had finally found peace. Before long, rather than renovating the castle – her ostensible reason for being there – she turned her attention to restoring the neglected gardens of Nassenheide. Her diaries detail the shrubs, flowers and seeds that she ordered and paid for out of her pin money, including ten pounds' worth of morning glory seeds.

In a letter to her father she wrote: 'Yes, indeed I am blessed, for I have found the kingdom of heaven, found by so few ... I have found the Lord but instead of having Him in a chapel I have found Him in my garden!'

Soon enough Elizabeth's husband interrupted her blissful sojourn:

The first part of that time of blessedness was the most perfect, for I had not a thought of anything but the peace and beauty all round me. Then he appeared suddenly who has a right to appear when and how he will and rebuked me for never having written, and when I told him that I had been literally too happy to think of writing he seemed to take it as a reflection on himself that I could be happy alone. I took him round the garden along the new paths I had made ... and he said that it was the purest selfishness to enjoy myself when neither he nor the offspring were with me ...

Henning found his wife's explanation impossible to comprehend. How could a woman be happy without her husband and children? Elizabeth tried to humour him but: 'Nothing appeased the Man of Wrath and he said he would go straight back to the neglected family.'

Afterwards Elizabeth recounts that she was:

disturbed by twinges of conscience ... whenever I found myself wanting to jump for joy ... but I could not manage to fret and yearn. What are you to do if your conscience is clear and your liver in order and the sun is shining?

Despite her twinges, she refused to allow anxiety to ruin her happiness. What modern mother of three small children, perpetually bombarded with Instagram images of immaculate

mums and bubs, best-practice yet impossible-to-live-up-to
parenting advice and fear-mongering about pederasts on every
street corner could permit herself such freedom? How many of
us, in this day and age, can boast such powers of detachment and
serenity? Or find such joy in simply having a clear conscience, a
clean liver and a little sunshine?

> Wise people want so many things before they can
> even begin to enjoy themselves, and I feel perpetually
> apologetic when with them, for only being able to offer
> them that which I love best myself – apologetic, and
> ashamed of being so easily contented.

Elizabeth returned to Berlin to convince her family to join her
at Nassenheide and partly succeeded. Henning relented but
only on the condition that he maintain the Berlin apartment.
On arrival at the country estate in May, he immediately took to
his bed, claiming to be ill. This illness, descending the moment
they arrived, seems indicative of the power play within the
marriage and Henning's continued attempt to remain his wife's
focus of attention. By the end of the month, however, he had
recovered and Elizabeth noted in her diary:

> This month has been a very blessed one in spite of H,
> and I can't express the love and grace and fellowship
> that is with me whenever I go into my garden (which
> has grown to be the presence of God to me). It is a
> benediction every time I go into it and there alone

I feel the same!

38

can I realise what is meant by the peace that passes all
understanding.

Elizabeth continued with renovating the house and settling in, while Henning spent as much time in the Berlin apartment as he did at Nassenheide, and his visits to the estate invariably aroused conflict. She began to think about escaping to England, if only for a holiday, and soon found an excuse to go. Her brother was getting married and Elizabeth wrote to Henning in Berlin asking permission to go to England for the wedding. He refused. On his next trip to Nassenheide, she met her husband at the station and tried again to convince him. That evening 'disgraceful scenes' ensued. The day before the wedding, Elizabeth attempted to leave without his permission but failed. 'H. furious,' she wrote in her diary, 'so can't go'. The next morning Elizabeth packed her bags and in defiance of her husband she ordered a carriage that Henning sent away again. That night she resolved to take the only way of escape left to her by stealing out of the house and walking ten miles to the station in the dark.

For her first week in England, Elizabeth's diary simply records the word 'happy'. Six weeks later, when her husband came to London, presumably to retrieve his runaway bride, she remained resistant to returning to Pomerania. The couple didn't leave until three months later and only after serious negotiations. Harmony in the relationship was restored, claims daughter Liebet, because of Henning's acquiescence, 'obtained we know not how or when' to his wife's insistence on residing at Nassenheide permanently. Even then, on departure from London, Elizabeth was 'tearful but resigned'.

Elizabeth's escape to England had afforded her a period of happiness. Escape, often covert and unauthorised, is a constant theme in her books; the women in her novels are frequently in flight, fleeing from men and towards freedom in pursuit of happiness. I can't help wondering whether this first, spectacularly risky and rebellious escape to England was possibly an attempt to separate from Henning permanently. The boldness of such action at that time, within that society, demonstrates a bravery that few women would have been able to muster. What courage it must have taken to not only abandon her husband but also her children.

Elizabeth's daughter, Liebet, later wrote about the effect on the three sisters of their mother's 'increasingly frequent and often dreadfully sudden disappearances to England' which 'clouded their sunny days in anticipation and left them utterly stricken when they occurred'. According to Deborah Kellaway, 'her children longed for her company but [eventually] accepted her withdrawal from them'. The nature of being a writer, which requires long periods of solitude, is clearly not compatible with being the ideal on-call and always-available mother.

On arrival back to Nassenheide in 1897, Elizabeth rejuvenated her stout-hearted temperament and continued with the renovations of her remote castle. In September, the family dined in the newly decorated dining room for the first time. A month later, Elizabeth's favourite room, the library, was finished in white and yellow and looked, she commented, 'so cheerful as to be almost frivolous'. The windows opened out on her most cherished part of the garden and the room was warmed in winter with a big fireplace.

By October, the word 'slaving', used often in her journal in relation to household duties and renovations, had disappeared. By December she was busy preparing for Christmas. As the local Countess, she was expected to give presents to all the locals as well as the house staff. She wrote: 'the preparations devolved entirely on me, and it is not very easy work, with so many people in our own house and on each of the farms, and all the children, big and little expecting their share of happiness'.

Perhaps the greatest advantage of residing at Nassenheide was that Elizabeth finally found the freedom to properly indulge her impulse to put pen to paper. On 7 May 1897, her journal reads: 'Began to write "In a German Garden", sitting among the raindrops and owls.' And ends with one final brief remark: 'H. cross.'

Henning was still pressuring her to produce an heir and in July 1897, Elizabeth noted in her diary: 'H and I quarrelled, he wanting a baby and I not seeing it.' Four days later she added: 'H. left for Berlin. Great relief and blessing.'

By September, Elizabeth is feeling so desperate that she wrote to her sister, Charlotte, whom she nicknamed 'Tit', asking if she could come and stay with her. Her diary then records: 'Got a telegram from darling Titter telling me to come.' This particular escape was postponed, however, by the arrival of her father who helped smooth things over between the couple. According to daughter Liebet, the apparent patching up of the relationship wasn't a genuine reconciliation but rather 'something like an armed truce'. Henning continued in his insistence that he needed a boy to perpetuate the von Arnim name, while for Elizabeth, 'his apparent willingness to sacrifice her happiness in such a cause was as unintelligible as it was repugnant'. For the rest of the month, she remained busy with household duties and children, only managing to return to her fledgling manuscript briefly.

Throughout spring Elizabeth busied herself outdoors, supervising the planting in an effort to achieve her vision of a 'natural' garden. (In January of that year she had read a book that may have inspired her – *The Garden That I Love* by Alfred Austin who was then poet laureate – in which the style was conversational and the attitude towards gardening unconventional.)

Upon sowing her first seeds, Elizabeth 'then waited in great agitation for the promised paradise to appear. It did not, and I learned my first lesson.' She writes realistically about the difficulties and disappointments of gardening, her many failures as well as her triumphs. She struggles with communicating her ideas of a 'natural' look to her gardeners, expressing her opposition to rows and formal beds:

... he went about with a long piece of string making parallel lines down the borders of beautiful exactitude and arranging the poor plants like soldiers at a review. Two long borders were done during my absence one day, and when I explained that I should like the third to have plants in groups and not in lines, and that what I wanted was a natural effect with no bare spaces of earth to be seen, he looked even more gloomily hopeless than usual ...

On this occasion, as on many others, Elizabeth's wishes were ignored. The fact that, as a Countess, she wasn't allowed to simply plunge her own hands into the earth and arrange her garden to her own desires, was a constant frustration.

If I could only dig and plant myself! How much easier, besides being so fascinating, to make your own holes exactly where you want them and put in your plants exactly as you choose ... I did one warm Sunday ... slink out with a spade and a rake and feverishly dig a little piece of ground and break it up and sow surreptitious ipomaea and run back very hot and guilty into the house and get into a chair and behind a book and look languid just in time to save my reputation ... it is a blessed sort of work, and if Eve had had a spade in Paradise and known what to do with it, we should not have had all that sad business with the apple.

As always, Elizabeth somehow transformed her frustrations into comedy. She could take the most unpromising material – unimaginative gardeners, oppressed wives, bad-tempered husbands – and make it funny. And that seems to me like a kind of literary alchemy, akin to transforming mud into gold, a talent that I'm also convinced she could apply to real life.

My research trip to England revealed little. Or, at least, little of the kind of revelations I was after. I wasn't chasing the day-to-day details of Elizabeth von Arnim's frantically crowded life; a catalogue of her comings and goings was not the kind of biography I was interested in writing.

My quest was about how to understand Elizabeth's temperament and her way of seeing things, how she maintained such buoyancy, such apparent relish of daily living. The journals are full of simple, quotidian pleasures:

> Lovely day with fat clouds sailing ...
> Picknicked and meditated in perfect peace and happiness ...
> Sweet day after rain. Biked am and meditated in garden ... Divine sunset cycling home ...
> In heavenliest and sublime warmth. The lupin hills against blue sky, the flowery hedges and grapes a dream. Felt as though I should burst for sheer happiness ...

What, I kept wondering, was the secret to her enviable ability to *enjoy* life? Not, of course, every waking hour, but for moments that seem so intense as to be positively transcendent.

Before travelling to England to do my Elizabeth research, I had made a short trip to Perth to visit relatives. While there I purchased a packet of seeds from the magnificent King's Park in the hope of planting a little bit of Western Australia in my own garden. My parents and grandparents grew up in Western Australia and I'd always felt I belonged there, that I was somehow out of place in Sydney. I thought perhaps if I could cultivate a tiny Western Australian garden on the east coast it would make me feel more at home. I had seen yellow everlasting daisies in bloom and longed to see them flower in my small Sydney patch. Armed with seed-raising mix and detailed instructions on how to coax these little daisies into existence, I gently sowed them and tended them daily. I knew that, being Western Australian, they hated humidity and preferred sandy soil, so after they raised their little heads I transplanted a row of tiny plants in a special propagating sand along the length of my picket fence. If everything went to plan, on arrival to my house visitors would be greeted by a blaze of bright yellow daisies that would, like their namesake, last and last. Every two days, as instructed, I gently showered my seedlings with a brief spray of water; too much would make them shrivel. And then I watched with nervousness and excitement as they grew stronger and taller, eventually developing into leafy bushes.

GABRIELLE CAREY

Finally, on the morning I left for my flight to London, I noticed a miracle: my everlastings were covered with tiny buds!

This was what I was looking forward to most on my arrival back into Sydney after a twenty-six-hour flight in an economy seat with an economy airline – being greeted by the cheerful faces of those sweet yellow daisies. But when the taxi turned into my cul-de-sac there was not a single flower in sight. The lawn mowing man had mistaken them for weeds and mowed every one of them down, buds and all. My everlastings were completely gone.

At the sight of the devastation, all my many years of frustration with the distorted male view of the world came to the surface. How is it possible not to distinguish between wilting weeds and flowers about to burst into bloom? How could anyone be so blind?

The fact that Elizabeth suffered similar disappointments at the hands of her male gardening assistants consoled me a little. I have since learnt that much of the world is comprised of people oblivious to the beauty of flowers, and even more insensible to the shy, unopened bud. The term 'plant blindness' is a condition discussed in scholarly journals and one of the principal reasons, according to the climate commentators, that humanity is facing ecological extinction: simply because so many of us lack the capacity that Elizabeth had in abundance – an ability to see the beauty that so bountifully surrounds us.

When not preoccupied with her plants, Elizabeth retreated to the room she had reserved for writing, spending long hours locked away from her family. The fact that she spent more time writing and less housekeeping was not kept hidden from her husband, but neither was Henning's irritation at having a writer for a wife.

In February of 1898 she noted of her writing progress, 'Nearly finished "G.G".' Later she felt obliged to show her manuscript to Henning – whom she refers to throughout as the 'Man of Wrath'. He was unhappy with what he read and ordered that the passages be expunged. That night Elizabeth went to bed in a rage and the next day, according to her journal, 'Struggled at altering "G.G" – felt intensely irritable and desperate about it.' But she was also obedient. In those days, German women and wives were not supposed to have opinions and they certainly were not supposed to have opinions that differed from their husbands and record them in writing. She accordingly re-wrote the censored sections before finally submitting her first completed work to Macmillan publishers.

Elizabeth was thirty-one when she posted off her manuscript entitled *Elizabeth and her German Garden* in the hope of becoming an author. While waiting for an answer, like so many writers, she fell into a deep depression, and her diary includes phrases such as 'wondered why I was born' and 'horridly depressed'. Then in March 1898, her journal entry begins as always, with a comment on the weather: 'Cloudy, windy and warm.' And ends briefly and unemotionally: 'Got answer re G.G. accepting it.'

Years later, as a seventy-year-old woman, Elizabeth re-read her diaries and wondered at her younger self's apparent reluctance to celebrate the achievement she'd so longed for: 'I vividly remember my heavenly happiness that day at the family luncheon, hugging my secret. I think this was perhaps the most purely happy moment of my life and I make no comment.'

Elizabeth's journal records the summer of 1898 as one of continuous joy. In June she 'Got up at 2.45 am and went in garden and saw sun rising over the rye fields. A unique and wonderful experience.' And then in July, 'Heavenly radiant hot still summer's day … lay on grass and watched the clouds.' And 'Meditated lying on grass all morning … tea under acacia … perfect afternoon. Evening in garden in lovely moonlight.'

This rapturous happiness appears to be in response to the weather and landscape but perhaps she was also bursting with happiness because she had at last found a way to express herself: her joyous personality was going to be communicated from her remote castle to thousands upon thousands of grateful readers across the world. Her voice would finally be heard.

The excitement about her first book was not the excitement of many a young contemporary writer. There would be no interviews or profiles or media interviews; Elizabeth was not looking forward to being a literary celebrity. Just the opposite. She was emphatic with her publishers that she wanted the forthcoming book to be published anonymously. So on receiving the proofs, she became alarmed that her request, perhaps like her requests to her gardeners, had been ignored.

Dear Sir,

I return the proof of the title page of my book and must earnestly beg you that my name is <u>omitted</u>. I should like to see a revised proof of the title page and that the book shall be, as you promised, <u>strictly</u> anonymous. I was surprised to see that in spite of our correspondence on this point my name appears on the title page. We had agreed that no name whatever was to appear and I must beg you to keep to this agreement. I am confident that you will carefully keep what must be, for family reasons, a secret.

The first pseudonym Elizabeth suggested to her publisher was 'Elizabeth Careless' – possibly because this was an adjective her husband used to describe her performance as a housekeeper. (She was later to develop the idea of the 'careless' wife who is not attentive enough to her household, transforming her husband's criticism into material for satire.) Her publisher, however, objected to the suggested surname so it was then shortened to Elizabeth. It is uncertain why she chose this name but likely that she was thinking of her own mother, known to all as Louey. Or even her cousin by marriage, the scandalous writer Elisabeth von Heyking, only five years older than Elizabeth, who had already shocked German society by having an affair that had resulted in her husband committing suicide, and later becoming a writer and author of the best-selling *Letters that Never Reached Him*. As with so many aspects of Elizabeth's life and personality, we will never know for sure what motivated her choice for a pen-name.

By mid-1898, Elizabeth was spending many hours a day writing in her upstairs room at Nassenheide, hard at work on her second book. On 15 July 1898, she recorded: 'Lovely day. Biked a.m. Began "The Solitary Summer" p.m. shut up in room. Biked after tea.'

This intense devotion to her writing led to, or at least coincided with, more conflict between herself and Henning, who was resentful that she was insisting on a room of her own. In August she notes in her diary: 'Had a row with H of a fairly disgraceful nature – didn't speak to each other all day (nor for many days afterwards).'

By the end of that month, relations hadn't improved when she notes, on the day she turned thirty-two: 'Birthday disappointing and H very cross.'

Arguments over heir-bearing worsened after the publication of *Elizabeth and her German Garden* in September1898. On 20 September her journal remarks: 'Grey, cold, windy. Stayed in all day reading. (G.G. came out.)' Her parenthetical announcement of such a momentous event might indicate her own superficially dismissive attitude to her own achievement. Or possibly suggests that it was something to be kept to herself, as a private celebration. Or do the brackets represent a boundary, protecting a secret place where her 'other life' resided?

Whatever clandestine self-congratulating may have happened didn't last long. The following week, scrawled vertically over the dates of 26, 27 and 28 September, there is an inky, smudged entry, possibly penned while still in a rage: 'Rows with H.' As usual, the reason for their rows is not specified. It is possible that, as well as the procreation argument, the couple were also quarrelling about the potential income that Elizabeth would receive from her newly published book. Under German law at the time, any income Elizabeth received would belong to her husband. Perhaps they were trapped in that perpetual double-act of marital disagreement: sex and money.

Elizabeth and her German Garden was immediately received with delight by reviewers and audiences alike and there was much discussion about the identity of this fresh new literary talent. Within three months of publication, Elizabeth's first book had been reprinted eleven times, earning the author 10,000 pounds, the equivalent of half a million sterling today. Almost overnight, she became one of England's favourite writers.

So what exactly was the appeal? There is no plot, no conflict, no character development (unless the garden is considered a character), no revelations, no sex, no crime and no twist at the end. It begins with: 'I love my garden,' and ends with something like a prayer:

I do sincerely trust that the benediction that is always awaiting me in my garden may by degrees be more deserved, and that I may grow in grace, and patience, and cheerfulness, just like the happy flowers I so much love.

Being a gardener might help a reader to enjoy Elizabeth's first best-selling book but it's certainly not essential. It's the personality that the reader engages with, a person able to see beauty and joy, and when the uglier side of life appears, as it must, utilises her astonishing 'comic detachment of mind' to satirise. Elizabeth Jane Howard comments that von Arnim's first book has 'a freshness, a freakish charm, an irrepressible energy that springs straight from the very source of her personality'. A more recent critic has observed: 'Her personality sold books; there was nothing else in them.'

In other words, the appeal was not the narrative but the character of Elizabeth herself: playful, witty and often so in awe of nature that she regularly falls into ecstatic rapture. Readers were seduced by her unusual ability to portray happiness at the same time as making them laugh, a very rare combination in a writer. Every few pages there is a reference to being happy or the state of happiness and she excels in describing different kinds of happiness, reminding us that being happy is not necessarily monotone – that there is an entire spectrum, a complete rainbow of shades of happiness. As a lover of all kinds of weather, Elizabeth celebrates each season, writing that:

... my spring happiness bears no resemblance to my summer or autumn happiness, though it is not more intense, and there were days last winter when I danced for sheer joy out in my frost-bound garden in spite of my years and children. But I did it behind a bush, having a due regard for the decencies.

This last flourish is typical of Elizabeth's playful attitude to conventions because she both believes and disbelieves what she says. Being a child of the late Victorian generation transplanted into the ultra-formal German aristocracy, Elizabeth was a diligent observer of a strict etiquette unimaginable nowadays, but in many ways she also disregarded the so-called common decencies. Even though she appeared on the surface as highly respectable, she regularly rebelled against the prevailing rules regarding proper womanly deportment.

'While the "novel" appears to be an ode to nature; within that ode is a determined rebellion,' notes Elizabeth Jane Howard of von Arnim's first book. 'Within this idyll of pantheism, she smuggles in ideas that rebel against the position of women and girls, but does so charmingly that few noticed how radical she really was.'

On the surface, *Elizabeth and her German Garden* looks like a book about gardening and yet within it the author bluntly and boldly inserts statements such as: 'I don't think a husband is at all a good thing for a girl to have.' And then, in reference to her three daughters, claims:

I shall do my best in the years at my disposal to train them so to love the garden, and outdoor life, and even farming, that, if they have a spark of their mother in them, they will want and ask for nothing better.

She is endorsing female independence, even the idea of women of the upper-class becoming farmers, and yet her playful tone avoids repercussions for these revolutionary remarks. Another commentator has observed: 'Though she had embarked on a serious critique of the institution of marriage, the book had a light, teasing tone; it was a charming birdcall of a protest.'

In the introduction to the Virago edition of *Elizabeth and her German Garden*, Elizabeth Jane Howard says:

> ...the singular aspect of this book is the author's determination to be something more than a good German wife and mother, and it is this quality, set against the more traditionally romantic hymn to nature that gives the work its unique flavour.

It is clear that Elizabeth was regularly angered by the strictures placed on her as a woman but her style of rebellion was creative and celebratory, rather than resentful and angry. Her rebellion was hidden, like her dancing behind a bush. At the same time as admirably playing the part of a Countess, she wrote a book in opposition to her husband and in which he is only referred to as the 'Man of Wrath'. While accepting the authority of the Count, she encouraged her daughters to think that husbands were not altogether necessary; and while she regularly suffered through the long formal German lunches of interminable courses, she also often escaped to the garden to picnic on salad instead – a joyous, rather than a scowling, rebel.

Soon after publication of *Elizabeth and her German Garden*, the *Daily Mail* produced a full page of speculations about the identity of the author 'Elizabeth', suggesting three possibilities: Queen Victoria's granddaughter Princess Henry of Prussia or Daisy, Princess Pless, or Countess Mary von Arnim. In response, Elizabeth became alarmed that her secret might be revealed and wrote to her publisher.

> Dear Sir,
> My friends, of course, have only to read this book to see that I must have written it, but it surely is possible to keep the authorship from the <u>general</u> public, and especially from the newspapers. If you will kindly continue to keep the secret I shall be able to do so too, and at least will be in a position to deny that I wrote it, as I should not hesitate to do if necessary.
> I remain, yours faithfully,
> C. von Arnim

Why did this secret so urgently need to be kept? In a previous letter she had cited 'for family reasons' but what does that mean exactly? For reasons owing to her disapproving husband? Of the extended von Arnim family? Of the family's reputation in *Junker* society? For the reason that a lady novelist would bring shame to the family? Were they opposed to countesses writing novels per se, or to countesses writing novels for money?

Later, when the requests for translation rights flooded in, all were happily granted, *except* for the translation rights into German. From this it can be assumed that Elizabeth's concerns about anonymity were particularly local. Scholar Isobel Maddison believes that her refusal to publish in Germany may also have been because the novel 'knowingly extended small-scale private, domestic matters to developing international concerns' arguing that her 'numerous satirical swipes at all classes of German people, intensify the sense that von Arnim was arguing for the clear-sighted recognition of an emerging, collective and militaristic German consciousness that was mobilising for war'.

On the other hand, the reason might have been purely personal. It is possible that during the editing process Elizabeth had re-inserted the parts of the manuscript that had been censored by her husband and her main concern of a German edition was the fear of her husband reading the published, rather than the draft version. It is also possible that she was again dissimulating and using the excuse of her family to maintain anonymity within her immediate Prussian society purely for her own sake. And that she was doing this because she instinctively understood that privacy was essential for happiness.

As I peered further and further into this extraordinary woman's life I was beginning to wonder whether it would ever be possible to uncover the unguarded, uncomposed – the 'real' Elizabeth – even in what was left of her diaries. I suspected that she knew that people like me would be raking over her remains, desperately hoping for some insight into her soul. But taking care of her soul, as she described it – which included protecting it from prying eyes of biographers – was her most important mission. This was why she was often seen as egotistical or smug or selfish – even 'inhumanly so', according to one reviewer. But this insistence on keeping her most private self private is also, I have come to believe, related to her remarkable capacity for happiness. Why and how, I was yet to discover.

Happiness Principle Number Two:
🌿 *Privacy*

In the wake of her first publishing success, Elizabeth records: 'Went to England alone.' On the day of her arrival, there was 'great jubilation' over the reunion with her family and then again the next day, in response to a glowing review of *Elizabeth and her German Garden* in *The Scotsman*.

Celebrations soon gave way to realities and Elizabeth's relatives set out to convince her that bearing a son for the sake of the von Arnim lineage was a duty she could not resile from. Later she wrote: (Relatives) are like drugs, useful *Amen!* sometimes, and even pleasant if taken in small quantities and seldom, but dreadfully pernicious on the whole and the truly wise avoid them.'

It is probable, however, that she was convinced by their arguments because soon after returning to Nassenheide she found she was pregnant again and 'suffering the dark forebodings and tendency to make Wills which always went with that condition'. Throughout the winter she continued to work on *The Solitary Summer*, and by the end of January 1899 reflected: 'Read it through – mixed feelings – chiefly disgust. Futility that cannot be uttered. Am, after all, a poor fool.' Elizabeth always considered her literary ability as 'a slender little talent'.

Given the weather at Nassenheide that year – lashing storms and fog that shrouded the estate, it is possible that Elizabeth's 'winter happiness' momentarily escaped her. Relations with Henning continued to be fractious and during this period she records her personal experience of one of the constant underlying themes of her novels: domestic violence.

I had quarrelled with H. I was sitting in a trousseau chemise, locked into the little pink room … and H. tried to get in. I was working on The Solitary Summer. When he found the door locked, and me silent as a fish, he went round into the next room, which had a communicating door, and tried that and burst it open. I was sitting at the writing table facing it. He picked up one of those big pencils they call a Bismarck Stift and hurled it at me. It missed me. I sat frozen with fury and didn't move, didn't speak and inscribed the date in the Nuttall dictionary open before me, so as never to forget.

There is something about this incident that captures all the elements that make up the dilemma of marriage for the woman writer: the constant desire for solitude and her failure to achieve it; the broken attempt at privacy; the assault by her husband with the very instrument she utilises to build her independent sense of self; the anger she cannot express and the self-imposed silence. The act of recording the date of the incident is Elizabeth's only defence. Nobody else has observed this event so she must be her own eyewitness. This is one of the reasons why she feels compelled to write: out of an angry desire for justice and a need to bear witness.

🌿

It was exactly this motive that had compelled me to sit down and write my first book, *Puberty Blues*: anger towards the surfie boys and a need to record an untold truth about teenage sexual violence. And Elizabeth's frequently fractious relationship with her husband is a situation I understand only too well. Throughout my life I have continuously tried and failed at the business of being a wife, each relationship riddled with conflict, and beset by scenes. Certainly, I have had the experience of partners who, like the Count, tried to beat down my study door because they were jealous of the devotion I gave to my writing, convinced that my vocation was the equivalent to a rival lover, constantly consuming my time and my thoughts. Indeed, sometimes I wonder if I hadn't been a writer, I may well have been able to be a wife. Maybe the two things are simply incompatible.

Would it have been any easier – for me, for Elizabeth, for creative women the world over – if we weren't cursed with a compulsion to write? Does such a calling compete with the role of wifely companion and mother? If I succeed at writing will I inevitably fail at marriage? And was I compelled to write in the first place because I had no voice? If I did feel heard would I lose the overwhelming urge to put pen to paper? Because that's often the motivation behind writing books – at least according to American writer Joan Didion – a desire to lock someone in a room and force them to listen.

I used to think it was all their fault: the men. They weren't smart enough, sensitive enough, sexy enough. The next one would be better, I thought. Now I wonder if claiming a higher (literary) calling may be just a high-minded excuse for my own very basic, very human failings – my avoidance of intimacy, my aversion to vulnerability, my intoxication with high romantic love and my boredom with lowly domestic day-to-day cohabitation, my incessant desire for the new and the novel, my own fickleness and inconstancy.

But perhaps the very idea of love is also to blame: the love as portrayed in traditional novels, in romantic poetry, in legends. As Elizabeth noted, the problem with romantic love is that it is unsustainable; it starts on such a high that after the initial rapture there is only one way it can go.

It is easy to get the impression that Elizabeth's marriage to Henning, like so many marriages, was a continual downward trajectory. But there is also evidence of genuine affection and by the time of publication of *The Solitary Summer* her mood had changed. The dedication reads: 'To the Man of Wrath with some apologies and much love.'

🌿

A common descriptor of Elizabeth's work is 'light' and 'middle-brow'. These days she is construed as a competent writer but not a serious one, possibly because she doesn't appear to confront the social and political 'issues' that our contemporary culture has somehow come to believe literature is obliged to expound. Note how many fellowships and residencies are now dependent on the writer/artist choosing a subject deemed worthy – such as climate change or racism. The non-fiction fellowship at the US Carey Institute for Global Good, for example, is 'particularly interested in supporting projects that examine the most pressing issues of the day' such as 'inequality, social justice, disability and intersectionality'. (Apparently good literature, on its own, is incapable of contributing to global good.) Similarly, the Bellagio Literary Arts Residency prefers proposals that 'promote the well-being of humanity, particularly through issues that have a direct impact on the lives of poor and vulnerable populations around the world'.

Of course, Elizabeth spent none of her professional life applying for residencies or grants or fellowships. If she wanted to go to Lake Como, she simply went. In fact, just after she turned sixty, she travelled to Bellagio with her friend Maud Ritchie to see the Serbelloni Gardens. 'Walked for two hours in a trance of beauty and happiness,' she recorded in her journal, '... we took a boat and rowed to Varenna and dined at the Victoria ... Back by moonlight. An enchantment!'

Right up to the last few weeks of her life, Elizabeth remained a seeker of enchanted places, usually gardens, and was a firm believer in the possibility of enchantment, a notion that is so foreign to us now that the word itself has just about disappeared from use.

Me too!

Elizabeth von Arnim's works can have the appearance of being light and frothy but only to a person who doesn't read deeply. Beyond her playful style is a serious critique of gender relations, surely one of the most important and pressing social issues of our times. Indeed, it is strange that she is not recognised as one of the earliest and acutest literary exposers of psychological and domestic violence against women. Even in *Elizabeth and her German Garden*, an ode to flowers and sunshine, there is one very disturbing episode that deals directly with domestic violence, a scene that is rarely referred to by commentators on her work, and that was completely ignored by reviewers at the time of publication.

The scene occurs when Elizabeth and her husband are out in a carriage riding together, an unusual event because while the narrator insists on going for regular excursions to enjoy the natural surroundings, her husband, she writes:

has no eye for nature ... and is simply bored by a long drive through a forest that does not belong to him; a single turnip on his own place is more admirable in his eyes than the tallest, pinkest, straightest pine.

While riding together they pass 'a batch of workers' including one woman working with a spade, despite the fact that she has only recently given birth.

> 'Poor, *poor* woman!' Elizabeth cries, suddenly feeling very angry. 'And her wretched husband ... will probably beat her tonight if his supper isn't right. What nonsense it is to talk about the equality of the sexes when the women have the babies!'

Her husband agrees that 'Nature' has assured there will never be equality, especially given that man 'has the brute force, and his last word on any subject could always be his fist'. He goes on to describe the 'commendable' habit of the 'lower classes everywhere ... to silence a woman's objections and aspirations by knocking her down'. He finishes his speech by saying that these women Elizabeth pities are rather to be envied 'since they are early taught, by the impossibility of argument with marital muscles, the impotence of female endeavour'.

It is a jarring experience for a reader enjoying a book brimming with rose gardens and happiness to be suddenly confronted with a blunt defence of domestic violence. Perhaps for this reason the passage is often ignored – it seems so out of place. It is likely that this speech from the Man of Wrath was based on an actual conversation and that acceptance of physical force in a marriage was entirely normal at the time, and that Elizabeth, in her usual subtle way, was trying to expose such practices. Her subsequent novels are full of instances of domestic tyranny, usually of the psychological rather than the physical kind, but no less damaging. In von Arnim's final book, *Mr Skeffington*, the protagonist, Fanny, reflects on a younger woman who has spent her life in slave-like service to her sanctimonious preacher brother:

> This worn-out woman two years younger than herself. How Miles must have banged her about. Not physically, of course, but there were lots of ways of banging a woman about without touching her. She could be overworked. She could be underfed. She could be out-talked, out-argued, preached at, set an example to ...

The 'lots of ways of banging a woman about without touching her' was one of Elizabeth's central topics. Her novels focus on the sort of domestic violence that is quietly insidious, often unseen and completely spiritually destructive. But although her villains may be maestros of tyranny, she is their equal in her virtuosic ability to expose them. The *Life* magazine article published when Elizabeth was seventy-three described her as an author who 'loves to impale lordly men with a deft touch of an entomologist mounting beetles'.

The following spring Elizabeth was again alarmed by the possibility of her real identity being made public. At the top of a letter to her publisher she glued a newspaper cutting which stated: 'The author of *Elizabeth and her German Garden,* who promises a new volume shortly, is said to be Miss May Beauchamp, now Countess von Arnim.'

> Dear Sir,
> I enclose a cutting from the 'Athenaeum' of April 1st. I wish to ask you whether it would be possible for you to contradict what they say. They have got my maiden name wrong, as it is Mary and not May, so that it could be contradicted truthfully as 'Miss May B' never existed. Could you not say that the statement that the book was written by the lady who before her marriage was M.M.B. is incorrect? I assure you this is giving me very great annoyance as after this in every review of the new book it will probably be mentioned. I should be greatly obliged if you could take advantage of the mistake in the name to contradict it, and let me beg you to advertise the new book only as by the author of "Elizabeth and her G.G."
> I remain etc.

For the rest of her long literary career, Elizabeth's books would appear with a title followed with: 'By the author of *Elizabeth and her German Garden*', a rather cumbersome nomenclature. But Elizabeth was convinced that her happiness and peace of mind depended on her ability to remain anonymous – an attitude that publishers generally abhor, even more so now. In contemporary times, an author who keeps a low profile, refuses media enquiries, declines interviews and shies away from publicity is usually an author who won't get past any publishing company's acquisition meetings. Elizabeth refused to engage with publicising her books and it wasn't until the very end of her life that she agreed to her first interview. And even then, she managed to deflect the attention onto her dog.

So what was it that Elizabeth understood about this mysterious relationship between anonymity and the ability to be happy? And if she was so cunning about keeping her secret secret, even posthumously, how was I ever going to find out?

The intimate relationship between happiness and privacy was driven home to me with force when, at the very outset of my research into Elizabeth's life, I discovered I had been the victim of identity theft. It was a long story that all started with my garden. I have always loved walled gardens and my own garden wall is a favourite feature of my backyard. I love the way the light falls on the clay-coloured bricks in the afternoon; I love how the height provides privacy; I love how it can be decorated with hanging baskets of petunias and climbing Pierre de Ronsard roses. But after many years, my garden wall began to fall down.

Just as I was planning to take up a poorly paid short-term fellowship interstate, the quote for the replacement wall came through: seventy thousand dollars. I felt winded at the sight of it. How was I going to maintain a house in Sydney and afford rent in another expensive city? I know! I thought, I would do what everyone else did: I would transform a company name into a verb and 'Airbnb' my home.

I was on the road when I received my first enquiry from 'Kaylah' – exactly halfway into the journey to the city that would be my home for the six-month duration of the fellowship. Kaylah and her family were looking for immediate temporary accommodation because they were renovating their home in a neighbouring suburb. My house was the perfect location, she said – close to her daughter's school. Could they check in?

The Airbnb app flashed me a message: 'You could earn $700 if you accept Kaylah's request!' Seven hundred dollars was exactly one-hundredth of the cost of a new garden wall. I had no other way to pay for it so perhaps this was the answer. Besides, wasn't this what everyone else did? And if everyone else did it, surely it wasn't completely immoral and unethical and wrong?

This was the thinking that led me to tell Kaylah that I would arrange for the keys to be left in my letterbox. This was also the thinking that led me to apologise for the fact that the porch was unswept. This was the thinking that encouraged me to tell them to make themselves at home, avail themselves of whatever was in the fridge and enjoy their stay. And yet something felt wrong.

The next day I asked my daughter to go over to my house and check if everything looked normal. She reported back that all the curtains were closed and the blinds were down. Two days later, my phone went dead and then my Gmail account was hacked. My instincts told me this had something to do with my so-called guests. Later I found out that while the blinds were down, 'Kaylah' had been busily rifling through my drawers and gathering all my essential details: credit card numbers, bank account details, birth certificate, passport – everything she and her crew needed in order to complete the identity theft was the use of my mobile number. This was easily done by ringing Vodafone, claiming to be me, offering a few personal details and asking for my number to be transferred from my old carrier. This, I later learnt, is called 'porting'.

The next part was straightforward: apply to banks for loans in my name. While waiting for approval, Kaylah and her gang continued to raid every corner of my house for anything of value, such as three vintage watches and a small stash of English pounds, and even for things I assumed were of no value at all: USBs containing manuscript drafts, handwritten letters from old lovers in the back of dusty drawers. There were no terrible secrets to be found in my filing cabinet or my hallstand or on my desk but a week later, when I realised the extent and nature of the robbery it felt profoundly different from the time I'd been robbed fifteen years earlier.

Violated is the word most commonly used to describe the experience of identity theft but that doesn't capture the sense of invasion and loss. It wasn't until much later that I realised I might be just as guilty as my home invader. 'The biographer at work is like the professional burglar,' says Janet Malcolm, 'breaking into a house, rifling through certain drawers that he has good reason to think contain the jewellery and money, and triumphantly bearing his loot away.' Kaylah may have ruthlessly robbed my identity, but was I equally heartless in my search for details of Elizabeth's life that she may well have preferred left undisclosed?

At the time of her first book's publication, Elizabeth was still Mary to her family and friends, and only Elizabeth to her readers. And that's the way she wanted it to stay, even, perhaps particularly, posthumously. The public face, in other words, should always remain completely separate from the private. Personal exposure of the contemporary kind where people reveal themselves totally, emotionally and physically via 'virtual platforms', would have horrified her. She instinctively understood the dangers of 'sharing' and the importance of privacy to the integrity of self. Perhaps she also understood that as long as your identity remains your own – and for her this meant remaining secret – it can't be stolen.

For Elizabeth, a person without secrets has lost their selfhood and therefore, having a secret, she implies, is essential to a secure sense of self. Yet keeping a secret, in the world of Facebook, Google and WhatsApp, has become close to impossible. And as long as we voluntarily offer up intimate details online, we are at risk of being hacked, and being hacked is anathema to secret-keeping – which is central – according to Elizabethan philosophy, to maintaining happiness.

Recently I was explaining to a group of young people over

69

lunch why I thought the crisis of privacy was just as much a threat to human existence as climate change. They looked at me doubtfully. If climate change is set to destroy us physically and environmentally, I argued, the inability to keep our inner thoughts and feelings from outside surveillance will destroy us psychically and psychologically.

At the end of the lunch one of the young women whipped out her phone to show us an image of her sister's ultrasound scan. She was excited about becoming an aunt and felt compelled to publicly celebrate the news. The phone was passed around so we could all gaze at the inside of the uterus of a woman we'd never met and admire a fetus the size of a blueberry, a tiny being who had only just sprouted appendages resembling hands and feet, and yet, at barely eight weeks into existence, was being surveilled in a café by strangers.

'Congratulations,' we said.

In June of 1899 Elizabeth and her husband travelled to England so she could give birth there, attended by her brother. At the end of July she produced her fourth daughter, the ill-starred and ironically named Felicitas. It appears the occasion resulted in more tears than joy. Afterwards, Elizabeth again experienced post-natal depression, and her thirty-third birthday was spent weeping 'without any apparent reason'. According to biographer Usborne, in order to put an end to her husband's insistence on an heir 'she contemplated drastic and unconventional action' but the details of the proposed action are unclear.

The couple and their new baby went back to Nassenheide in September, where much of the garden was in flower, and Elizabeth's spirits improved. Then three days after their return, Elizabeth's happy homecoming was interrupted by an event that the writer would remember with horror for the rest of her life. On the afternoon of 23 September 1899 she was in the drawing room reading when a footman entered and announced: 'Countess, they want to arrest the Count.'

The diary entry for that day begins, as any other, with the weather. 'Bright and windy,' and then follows with, 'H arrested after lunch and taken away to Stettin,' with no hint at the trauma she felt. The date became seared into her mind and her journals often remark on the anniversary of Henning's arrest. More than three decades later, in 1930, she recalled in her journal:

> H. was arrested in Nassenheide 31 years ago today. A windy sunny day and all the marigolds in flower. He was going shooting rabbits after lunch. Instead he went to prison. I remember every detail, even the clothes I had on.

Henning was taken away and imprisoned in the local town of Stettin where he was to stay on remand until his case came to court. He had been charged with embezzlement, an accusation made by the managers of a bank of which he was the director. The scandal of a titled man of property being gaoled was so great that friends and family could not be depended on

71

for help. Even Elizabeth's closest sister and father did not offer support and she was later to write that she felt utterly abandoned and alone.

It is typical of Elizabeth that during one of the most difficult periods of her life she was still able to produce work that was lighthearted and joyous. Throughout this testing time Elizabeth kept the fate of her husband secret from her daughters and continued to work on a new book for children, *The April Baby's Book of Tunes with the story of how they came to be written*, drawing on her considerable abilities for musical composition. The book opens:

> Once upon a time there were three little girls called April, May and June ... Luckily, the stork didn't bring any more babies after the June one, or I don't know what would have happened. How could you call a baby February, for instance? These babies lived in Germany, and that is why the stork brought them. In England you are dug up out of a parsley-bed, but in Germany you are brought by a stork, who flies through the air holding you in his beak, and you wriggle all the time like a little pink worm, and then he taps at the window of the house you are bound for, and puts you solemnly into the nice warm cushion that is sure to be ready for you, and you are rolled round and round in flannel things, and tied comfortably on to the cushion, and left to get your breath and collect your wits after the quick journey across the sky. That is exactly what happened to

April, and May, and June. They often told their mother about it, and said they could remember it quite well.

This book, which features narrative, illustrations and musical scores, beautifully reflects Elizabeth's extraordinary playfulness. The narrator, mother of the three 'babies' April, May and June, (Eva, Liebet and Trix), recounts the story of entertaining her children one wintry weekend by teaching them to sing English nursery rhymes to tunes Elizabeth herself composes. Presumably, some of the dialogue throughout was based on real conversations with her daughters.

Then the mother began to tell them about Miss Muffet, and of course the first question the babies asked was, 'What is a tuffet?' To which ... the mother replied, (who had gone to the length of examining the pages of *Nuttall's Pronouncing and Defining Dictionary* in search of enlightenment, and found that tuffets were left severely alone), 'A thing you sit on.'

'I thinks it must have been one sofa,' said June.

'A sofa?'

'Yes, else two people can't sit together on anything other than one sofa.'

'But there weren't two people.'

'Yes, the spider did sit beside her.'

'But a spider isn't people,' said April looking puzzled.

'Yes she is,' said June.

'No, she isn't,' said April ...

As well as teaching them songs, their mother arranges for each daughter to receive 'a lovely little pink letter' inviting them to afternoon tea. Seated around the fireplace in the library, they share a jug of chocolate and jam doughnuts after which their mother explains about a gardener called Mary who was so contrary that she pulled out all her flowers and replaced them with silver bells and cockle shells. It is unsurprising that her children missed their mother so badly during her regular 'sudden disappearances'.

Elizabeth's ability to continue with her creative life – composing songs and stories – while her material existence and marital wellbeing was under serious threat is testament to her extraordinary powers of detachment. It is almost impossible to understand how she could have written such a frivolous and funny book while simultaneously suffering the anxiety of her immediate reality. There is no way of ascertaining her real feelings at this time because her diary falls silent for months and is only resumed again on Henning's release, in July 1900, leaving us clueless about how she managed to maintain her good humour. But there is no doubt she contemplated the possibility of losing everything – her beloved Nassenheide, her garden, her esteemed reputation and her treasured privacy.

My conviction is that Elizabeth possessed, or had developed through necessity, an almost supernatural sense of detachment, a quality reflected repeatedly in her novels, that continually allowed her to see the comedy in situations that many of us would find intolerable. Her ability to rise above and detach from disruptive events is an example to us all, and a quality that I have come to believe is essential to happiness.

Happiness Principle Number Three:
🌿 *Detachment*

After a gruelling period of imprisonment and a lengthy, expensive trial paid for by his wife's literary earnings, Henning was cleared of all charges in 1901. The allegations had been false, trumped up by resentful colleagues. The diary is then resumed and Elizabeth continues her daily habit of noting, before anything else, the weather. As spring approaches the entries record the simple joy of daily life: 'Beautifully warm and bright ... All day in garden, reading and being happy. Tea on veranda. Plum-tree under south windows beginning to flower.'

Elizabeth resumed her writing with renewed energy, determined to establish a space where she could write in peace. A former orangery in the garden was converted into a studio known as the *Treibhaus*, described by the author as 'mouldy but quiet, as a commodious grave might be'. One biographer notes the symbolism of a child of the Southern Hemisphere taking shelter in a greenhouse, 'like an exotic plant' in order to 'flourish in an alien climate'.

The family as well as the servants were forbidden from disturbing Elizabeth in her garden refuge and above the door she had enscribed *Procule Est Profani*, which roughly translates to

'Begone, you who don't belong here'. The windows of the *Treibhaus* were deliberately kept unclean so no one could peer in.

Like so many women writers, Elizabeth established her retreat at a distance from her home because her attempts to write amid domesticity had been fraught and she was besieged with constant interruptions. Nobody, it seems, took her privacy or her writing projects seriously, especially Henning. This was despite the fact that her considerable earnings were essential to the maintenance of their life at Nassenheide. Nowhere have I found any evidence of her husband celebrating his wife's career or her success, even though he was eventually to become totally financially dependent on her.

At the *Treibhaus* only one person was allowed to enter. Once a day, at a fixed hour, the gardener came to fill the vases with fresh flowers and replenish the firewood. Inside was a big desk, a day bed, an easychair and bookshelves that lined the walls. Five years after arriving at Nassenheide, Elizabeth von Arnim had achieved what Virginia Woolf was to later proclaim as essential for every woman writer.

The April Baby's Book of Tunes, with its delightful illustrations by Kate Greenaway and accompanying music scores, was released for Christmas in 1900 and received critical as well as popular success. The *London Mercury* announced that 'the delightful author of *Elizabeth and her German Garden* (whose anonymity still puzzles us) treads in fresh fields and pastures in *The April Baby's Book of Tunes*'. The Dundee *Evening Telegraph* opens their review with the words: 'Elizabeth, whoever she is ...' And *The Sydney Morning Herald* review also refers to the mystery of the writer's identity: 'The author of *Elizabeth and her German Garden*, about whom so much interest has been excited, appears in a fresh light with *The April Baby's Book of Tunes.*' But the Melbourne magazine, *The Arena*, announces the arrival of the new book as follows: 'The Countess of Arnim, of Elizabeth of German Garden fame, has been engaged on *The April Baby Book of Tunes.*' Clearly, in some circles at least, Elizabeth's real identity was no longer a secret.

Elizabeth's way of expunging the experience of her husband being wrongfully imprisoned was to write her first novel proper, *The Benefactress*. (Her previous two books were written in first-person journal format and closer to memoir than fiction.) The opening sentence of *The Benefactress* announces the philosophical question at the heart of all of Elizabeth's books: 'whether the pleasure extractable from life at all counterbalanced the bother of it ...'

The story begins, like many of her subsequent novels, with a woman wanting to avoid marriage, suspecting that she is unsuited to the wifely role and desiring independence. When Anna Estcourt fortuitously inherits land and money from her German uncle, she plans to share it with twelve other women similar to her – husbandless through choice or loss – believing she can share her happiness as easily as she can share her fortune. Her heart is filled 'with tenderness for those who were not happy – for those who wasted their one precious life in being wretched when they might have been happy'. So, under the enforced guidance of the local parson – young, independent women could not be relied on to make sensible decisions – an advertisement is put in the paper:

> A Christian lady offers her home to others of her sex and station who are without means and without friends and without hope … She has room in her house in the country for twelve such ladies, and will be glad to share with them all that she possesses of fortune and happiness.

From the applicants Anna selects the 'Chosen'. But the experiment does not go according to her vision – reality clashing harshly with ideals – and towards the end of the novel the question is asked:

> What is the use of picking out unhappy persons well on in life, and thinking you are going to make them happy? How can you make them be happy? If it had been possible to their natures they would have been so long ago.

This seems to be integral to Elizabeth's philosophy of happiness: there are those who are more temperamentally inclined to happiness and those more inclined to melancholy. Those who do not have the capacity already in 'their natures' will not be happy, no matter how much is provided to them. Later she refines her philosophy:

> People are born in one of three classes: children of light, children of twilight, children of night. And how can they help into which class they are born? But I do think the twilight children can by diligence, by, if you like, prayer and fasting, come out of the dusk into a greater brightness. Only they must come out by themselves. There must be no pulling.

Anna's mistake in *The Benefactress* is her purposeful pulling, her insistence on rescuing and helping and trying to *make* other people happy. The novel concludes that, 'Five ought really to be the average age of the Chosen,' on the assumption that as we get older we inevitably become unhappier. Children have it in their natures to be happy and perhaps this means that, temperamentally, we all begin life with the ability to be happy. In another novel, *Fräulein Schmidt and Mr Anstruther*, Elizabeth comments:

> I could never be a schoolmistress I should be afraid to teach the children. They know more than I do. They know how to be happy, how to live from day to day in godlike indifference to what may come next. And is not how to be happy the secret we spend our lives trying to guess?

The quest at the centre of *The Benefactress* – that of attempting to provide the conditions in which a dozen middle-aged spinsters will be made happy – fails. The protagonist, Anna, comments at the end of the experiment:

> It seems so absurd that the only result of my trying to make people happy is to make every one, including myself, wretched. That is a waste, isn't it? Waste, I mean, of happiness. For I, at least, was happy before.

Like Henning, the heroine's love interest, Axel, is falsely accused of a crime and imprisoned, and like Elizabeth, Anna is obliged to negotiate with difficult, obstructive officials in order to visit him in an airless cell.

> The few hours he had thought to stay in that place were lengthening out into days ... a profound gloom was settling down on him. If no one helped him from outside, his case was indeed desperate ... Where were they all, those jovial companions who shot over his estate so often? The hours dragged by, each one a lifetime, each one so packed with opportunities for going mad, he thought, as he counted how many of them separated him already from his free, honourable past life.

Through the medium of the novel we learn of the real-life experience suffered by Elizabeth and Henning as she writes about her heroine's response to her lover's incarceration:

... everywhere was dismay and desolation ... All that had gone before part of a long sleep – a sleep disturbed by troubling and foolish dreams, but still only a sleep and only dreams. She woke up ... and remained wide awake after that for the rest of her life.

Was this perhaps the first time Elizabeth realised that she might have to assume the entire responsibility of the family and the estate, including the heavy financial burden? Was she foreseeing what was soon to become her reality?

Elizabeth's transition from her 'natural' first-person voice – employed in *Elizabeth and her German Garden* and *The Solitary Summer* – to the omniscient narrator of *The Benefactress* was not achieved without a struggle. Her first foray into fiction and away from diary form is very much the work of an apprentice novelist. The happy ending – with the Chosen leaving and being replaced by a husband – was not true to Elizabeth's philosophy or experience and she notes her difficulties in her diary: 'After tea rewrote tiresome love-scene in "Benefactress". Dislike love and loathe scenes.'

Later, on completing the manuscript, she reflected: 'Read *Benefactress* from beginning to end, and saw its weaknesses depressingly clearly. It is so ill-balanced – the first part too leisurely and the end so rapid ... I am done for I fear.' And yet, rather than falling into a typical writerly self-pity, she simply promises herself 'to try to do better next time'. Perhaps this was another advantage of writing anonymously; she didn't have to worry so much about her writerly profile or risk taking bad reviews personally. A pen-name offered protection.

According to the Usborne biography, another important event happened soon after the resolution of Henning's trial, when Nassenheide received a visit from the feminist Maude Stanley whose salons in London Elizabeth had attended. With Stanley's help, Usborne claims, Elizabeth negotiated a kind of 'post-nup' with her husband so that the income from her books thereon became her own. The education of her four daughters was also discussed at length, and Henning agreed that they should be educated like boys, 'as if there was no difference at all'. As part of the deal, they also came to an agreement that Elizabeth would be allowed to make annual visits to England.

Following these negotiations, says Usborne, Elizabeth 'was happy for the first time since her marriage to Henning' and was 'finally free of the intermittent depression that had dogged her for the past ten years'. But Usborne, like all commentators on Elizabeth's feelings (myself included), is only speculating. Elizabeth may not have been happily married – an exceedingly rare condition in my view – but her books and journals clearly demonstrate her capacity for intense happiness, an experience, I believe, that is impossible to fake.

The suggestion that this chronicler of happiness may also have suffered regularly and possibly deeply from depression doesn't surprise me. Elizabeth's diaries frequently record the word 'depression' but she tried hard not to inflict her gloom on others. If happiness was something she often enjoyed privately, depression was also something she believed should be borne individually. Unlike contemporary ideas about the importance of counselling and 'talk therapy', Elizabeth believed that sharing misery only increased the gloom and risked infecting others. Later in life, when questioned by her young lover about her withdrawal into silence, she responded: 'I just got into a trough of dejection and had difficulty in getting out, that's all.' She goes on to explain that she had written him a letter, 'but it was so gloomy that I didn't post it – why pour gloom over one's happy friends? I'm ashamed of having let you see a bit of it …'

Instead of seeking out expensive psychoanalysis or prescriptions for medication, when Elizabeth was depressed she sought healing in the gardens and forests that surrounded Nassenheide, as she notes in her diary directly after Henning's release from gaol: 'All afternoon in garden – so perfect – so blessed – so healing.'

This may be the only hint of the trauma that she was recovering from. If the garden was healing, there was obviously something to be healed from. And it certainly continued to offer therapeutic restoration. In May she writes:

Perfect day – the garden full of blossoms … cherry trees glorious, lilies of the valley in bud, forget-me-nots out – oh so lovely, so perfect, such a splendid, blissful world. Sat in garden among dandelions, too

happy to do anything but stare round – lilacs well on
the way to flowering.

What Elizabeth was undergoing would now be called
horticultural therapy. It seems obvious to those of us who love
gardens and flowers but the fact that sitting in beautiful green
spaces can be healing has now been recognised as so effective
it has led to a whole new therapeutic practice around gardens.
Horticultural therapists are now employed to create gardens in
hospitals and nursing homes. Instead of taking a pill, patients
sit in the sunshine among green leaves and budding flowers.
Gardening and growing things, researchers have confirmed,
leads to improved mental health. (Not exactly news to the
thousands of Australian gardeners who sit down every Friday
night to watch *Gardening Australia* ahead of their weekend of
pottering in the backyard.) Indeed, it has been found that
gardening can be more effective than a course of antidepressants.
In an essay 'Why We Need Gardens', Oliver Sacks remarks:

> I cannot say exactly how nature exerts its calming and
> organising effects on our brains, but I have seen in my
> patients the restorative and healing powers of nature
> and gardens, even for those who are deeply disabled
> neurologically. In many cases, gardens and nature are
> more powerful than medications.

The argument for nature as a powerful force for healing is also
reflected in the Shine Program, an initiative that encourages

doctors to write 'park prescriptions', which operates across thirty-four states in the United States. Instead of being offered pharmaceuticals, patients are given a schedule that involves a series of outings to parks, with some GPs prescribing outdoor prescriptions as often as they prescribe pills.

Elizabeth was well aware of the health benefits of being in nature, as her first two books attest. As usual, she was ahead of her time. It is encouraging to me, a person not in possession of such a gifted temperament for happiness as Elizabeth, to know that she also suffered periods of serious depression. It is also encouraging that, with the help of her greenhouse and her gardens, she recovered. Perhaps that means redemption is waiting just outside the door.

Happiness Principle Number Four:
🌿 *Nature and Gardens*

Despite Elizabeth's reservations, reviews of *The Benefactress* were mostly positive, several of them noticing similarities to Jane Austen, and *The Examiner* referring to her as 'The Unknown Genius' because the book appeared only as 'By the author of *Elizabeth and her German Garden*'. Her attempt to maintain her anonymity, it seems, was mostly succeeding, with a notable exception. On the other side of the world *The Australasian* announced that, 'The first effort in serious fiction by the author of *Elizabeth and her German Garden* and *A Solitary Summer* will receive a ready welcome from the thousands of readers who were charmed by those two works,' adding proudly that, 'in Australia the new book is entitled to a more than usually warm reception because as is now generally known, the gifted author is an Australian native.'

It is difficult to pinpoint exactly when Elizabeth transformed from 'The Unknown Genius' to the celebrity author who was recognised in London wherever she went. Over the next few years, her critical success as well as her sudden wealth eventually gave her the confidence to 'come out' and it is clear she hugely enjoyed her personal and professional popularity.

Not all the critics, however, were thrilled with Elizabeth's new novel. In England, the more serious London literary magazine, *The Athenaeum*, delivered a bad review and others talked about her work in terms of 'froth and trifles'. Elizabeth was beginning to realise that wit and humour in a novel could often mean it was precluded from being considered serious literature, and that tragedy and horror were more likely to find approval from heavyweight literary critics.

'If ever I write a second novel, which won't be ever, it shall be steeped to the top of its pages in blood,' she wrote. 'I might kill H in it and give a detailed account of how he looked disembowelled and call it *The Murder of the Man of Wrath.*'

If only she could have known just how prophetic she was being. What would Elizabeth have thought of our current fascination with 'torture porn' as a genre of storytelling? How would she have interpreted the popularity of *You Know You Want This* or *Wolf Creek*? Is there a point where audiences will grow tired of disembowelments and dystopias as entertainment and if so, what will replace them?

🌱

True to her time and place, Elizabeth was highly conscious of *Pflichten* – her duties. During the years spent at Nassenheide as mother and wife, notwithstanding her increasing success as a writer, household responsibilities still came first. Entire days could be taken up with organising the linen or supervising sausage-making. Often her writing time was limited to a few hours in the *Triebhaus* in the evening. But her nature, being simultaneously conservative and radical, also rebelled against duty, and she came to believe that the only way for her to survive – spiritually, emotionally, artistically – was to regularly take a break from responsibilities.

> It has been a conviction of mine that there is nothing so absolutely bracing for the soul as the frequent turning of one's back on duties. This was exactly what I was doing; and oh ye rigid female martyrs on the rack of daily exemplariness, ye unquestioning patient followers of paths that have been pointed out, if only you knew the wholesome joys of sometimes being less good!

In 1901 Elizabeth decided she would take a substantial break from her duties by travelling to the island of Rugen, a holiday that she also planned to use as material for her next book. She may have decided, after the difficulties of writing *The Benefactress*, that her strengths lay in non-fiction, or a kind of hybrid of journal and anecdote. This new book was to be part fiction and part travelogue. The intention was to make her escape a walking holiday. Elizabeth was a devoted walker and believed that it was the best way to observe the beauty of the world:

> It is the perfect way of moving if you want to see into the life of things. It is the one way of freedom. If you go to a place on anything but your own feet you are taken there too fast, and miss a thousand delicate joys that were waiting for you by the wayside.

Her plans, however, were thwarted because it was deemed impossible for a woman to walk alone.

> Round this island I wished to walk this summer, but no one would walk with me…The grim monster Conventionality whose iron claws are for ever on my shoulder, for ever pulling me back from the harmless and wholesome, put a stop to that.

A carriage, horses and a coachman were therefore decided as essential and in the summer of 1901 the author set out with ordinance maps to experience what would eventually become *The Adventures of Elizabeth in Rugen*.

Elizabeth's new book – part travelogue, part novel and part memoir – centres around two escaping women: Elizabeth, and her fictional cousin, Charlotte, possibly based on her relative by marriage, Elisabeth von Heyking. While Elizabeth is taking a holiday from home duties, Charlotte, the women's rights campaigner, is attempting to leave her husband, the much older and comically abstracted Professor.

Prior to the cousins meeting accidentally at a seaside resort, Elizabeth is more than content to be accompanied only by her driver, the long-suffering August, and her taciturn maid Gertrud. Her soul mate during this period is Wordsworth, the poet whose worship of the sublime reflected her own religious adoration of wilderness. In order to keep herself from floating away into rhapsody, she also carries a copy of Keats' 'Ode to Melancholy'. One sunny day, while picnicking on bread and butter and surrounded by yellow and purple nightshades, she feels her joy might be at risk of rising to intoxication and reaches for her volume of Keats.

Lest I should feel too happy, and therefore be less able to bear any shocks that might be awaiting me, I repeated the melancholy and beautiful ode for my admonishment under my breath.

> She dwells with Beauty—Beauty that must die;
> And Joy, whose hand is ever at his lips
> Bidding adieu; and aching Pleasure nigh,
> Turning to poison while the bee-mouth sips.

She laments, however, that the intended sobering effect of the poet's melancholy was not achieved:

> Usually it is an unfailing antidote in its extraordinary depression to any excess of cheerfulness; but the wood and the morning sun and the bread and butter were more than a match for it. No incantation of verse could make me believe that Joy's hand was for ever at his lips bidding adieu. Joy seemed to be sitting contentedly beside me sharing my bread and butter ...

One of Elizabeth's favourite indulgences was simply lying in the sun. The fact that the joy of lying idly in the sun inspires guilt in most people was another aspect of the human condition she enjoyed satirising. While holidaying, she notes the freedom of animals compared to the human experience, observing 'lizards, down at my feet, motionless in the hot sun, quite unaware of how wicked it becomes to lie in the sun doing nothing directly you wear clothes and have consciences'.

Elizabeth's ecstatic enjoyment of solitary picnics is put to an end when Charlotte assumes her cousin must be lonely and insists on accompanying her around Rugen. As they travel together, Elizabeth listens to Charlotte's lectures about the oppression of women and their right to rise up.

> Yes, she was right, nearly always right, in everything she said, and it was certainly meritorious to use one's strength, and health, and talents as she was doing,

trying to get rid of mouldy prejudices. I gathered what she was fighting for were equal rights and equal privileges for women and men alike. It is a story I have heard before, and up to now it has not had a satisfactory ending. And Charlotte was so small, and the world she defied was so big and so indifferent ... I protest that the thought of this brick wall of indifference with Charlotte hurling herself against it during all the years that might have been pleasant was so tragic to me that I was nearly tempted to try to please her by offering to come and hurl myself too. But I have no heroism. The hardness and coldness of bricks terrifies me.

Charlotte plays the principled, shrill feminist throughout *The Adventures of Elizabeth in Rugen* while the narrator gently mocks her earnestness. This doesn't mean the author has no sympathy for her position; in fact, Charlotte may well be a mouthpiece for views that Elizabeth preferred not to voice publicly. 'I could not but agree with much that she was saying,' admits Elizabeth when she first meets Charlotte.

Although we understand that Elizabeth has sympathy for her cousin, who is dedicated to writing pamphlets and giving lectures on the liberation of women, she also makes it clear that Charlotte's style and tone of protest is not to her taste. She does not, personally, enjoy being lectured to, especially while on holiday:

Of course I knew from the pamphlets and the lectures that she was not one to stay at home and see the point of purring over her husband's socks; but I had supposed one might lecture and write things without bringing the pamphlet manner to bear on one's own blood relations ... Now why could she not talk on this subject without being vehement? There is something about vehemence that freezes responsiveness out of me.

The difference between the cousins is that Elizabeth's preferred protest is in the form of irony rather than complaints and objections. She also realises that mockery is more effective and cleverly satirises Thomas Carlyle's then popular theory of 'The Great Man'.

If there are to be great men some one must be found to look after them – some one who shall be more patient, faithful, and admiring than a servant, and unable like a servant to throw up the situation on the least provocation. A wife is an admirable institution ... She attends to his bodily wants, and does not presume to share his spiritual excitements. In their common life he is the brain, she the willing hands and feet. It is perfectly fair.

Elizabeth is far more in agreement with Charlotte than her younger, disgruntled cousin realises. Her thoughts on the limitation of being a wife are absolutely clear:

She is the hedge set between the precious flowers of the male intellect and the sun and dust of sordid worries. She is the flannel that protects when the winds of routine are cold. She is the sheltering jam that makes the pills of life possible. She is buffer, comforter, and cook. And so long as she enjoys these various roles the arrangement is perfect. The difficulties begin when, defying Nature's teaching ... she refused to be the hedge, flannel, jam, buffer, comforter, and cook; and when she goes so far on the sulphuric path of rebellion as to insist on being clever on her own account and publicly, she has in Germany at least, set every law of religion and decency at defiance.

Elizabeth is clearly referring to herself here: she had defied 'Nature's teaching' and dared to be clever on her own account, counter to all the contemporary views in Prussia at that time. It is hardly surprising that she needed to get away for a holiday.

Charlotte implores her cousin to join her in the suffragette movement but Elizabeth – in the novel and in life – disapproved of blatant protest as 'too crude and obvious'; the very notion of public protest was antithetical to her treasured sense of privacy. Anything that exposed her to such an extent, physically as well as intellectually, would have caused her to cringe. It can also be surmised that another of Elizabeth's objections to the mainstream feminist movement of the time was aesthetic. Happiness, for her, was inextricably bound up with beauty. Her novels and her characters primarily find this beauty in nature, but the beauty of silk and lace, hats, dresses and shoes – along with all the other conventional feminine sensibilities – were also important. Photos of Elizabeth show a beautifully groomed woman, almost always adorned with a necklace; the utilitarian, earnest nature of cropped hair and bloomers held no appeal. For her own daughters she wished complete independence but also hoped for a certain measure of joyful, sensuous frivolousness.

> If I had a daughter I would bring her up with an eye fixed entirely on a husbandless future. She should be taught some trade as carefully as any boy. Her head should be filled with as much learning as it would conveniently hold side by side with a proper interest in ribbons.

'Ribbons' in this sense is literal but also symbolic of all that is traditionally feminine and traditionally denigrated by the world of men as superficial and insignificant. A proper interest in ribbons means, in part, an interest in frivolity and fun, the concrete and the sensual – rather than the abstract and the absolute. The very phrase 'a proper interest in ribbons' is a deliberate tease aimed at the seriousness of men. A proper interest in ribbons is an unashamed delight in colour and beauty but it does not equate, as some might assume, to a preoccupation with physical appearance. In fact, von Arnim's novels are curiously silent, for the most part, about what characters look like and the clothes they wear; her preoccupation with beauty cannot be accused of a superficial fixation with fashion.

What Elizabeth found intolerable was any philosophy of life or attitude that didn't encourage playfulness and joy and an aesthetic appreciation. For that reason, the suffragettes, who offered up their precious lives for the sake of their principles held no appeal. Elizabeth's objective was happiness and people who lived for their principles, she had noticed, were not happy. 'It is years since I have observed that the principled groan a good deal and make discontented criticisms of life, and I don't think I care to be one of them.'

The Adventures of Elizabeth in Rugen is a more explicit investigation of feminist ideas than the author had written previously. In it, Elizabeth offers a kind of feminism very different from the suffragette approach of her era – a form of female protest she considered particularly joyless, resulting in the emancipists leading *less* happy lives, and therefore only adding to their oppressive existences. She admired the heroism and nobility of the emancipists, agreeing with their objection to the status quo, but Elizabeth valued her own personal pursuit of happiness over a collective attempt at liberation.

In this book Elizabeth also makes clear another essential, and very modern ingredient in her recipe for happiness: the daily practice of physical exercise. No matter how busy, Elizabeth rarely allowed a day to pass without walking, hiking, mountaineering or cycling. She was clearly a woman of enormous energy who enjoyed the outdoors but not for the sake of her 'abs' or her 'glutes'; exercising was a way of nourishing her soul. During her travels around Rugen, she walked and swam every day of her ten-day holiday, reflecting on the after-effects of physical exertion:

> That evening was one of profound peace. I sat at my bedroom window, my body and soul in a perfect harmony of content. My body had been so much bathed and walked about all day that it was incapable of intruding its shadow on the light of the soul, and remained entirely quiescent, pleased to be left quiet and forgotten in an easy-chair.

Physical exercise is something I came to reluctantly and very late in life. At school, I loathed sport because it centred around competition. Nobody ever mentioned that playing hockey or football might make me feel better; the emphasis was on winning, being a team player and representing your school. In any case, the only sport I had any interest in – football – was not permitted for girls in the early 1970s. On weekends, which I spent almost exclusively at the beach, the physical activity that might have lifted my spirits – surfing – was also prohibited for girls. So by the time I got to adulthood, I had missed the opportunity to develop the habit of daily physical exercise. It wasn't until I was in my forties, during the aftermath of yet another major relationship breakdown, while suffering my first serious clinical depression requiring heavy-duty drugs, that I experienced the powerful uplifting effects of exercise. It's a simple habit that I have now come to believe was one of the keys to Elizabeth's 'habit of being happy inside'.

Happiness Principle Number Five:
🦋 *Physical Exercise*

On returning from Rugen, Elizabeth resumed a regular writing routine until her fertility once again got in the way. In March 1902 she noted: 'Full of forebodings of a horrible kind. Took a hot foot-bath but resultless.' A hot foot-bath was an attempt to bring on her period but the next day records: 'Fine day, but I in deep despair for reasons above. Could not write – spent a most wretched day.' The diaries then fell silent and her writing almost ceased. She sent her youngest daughter Felicitas to stay with her parents in order to have one less child to deal with – possibly the first sign of the fractious relationship which would eventually end in tragedy.

One biography claims that Elizabeth went to her doctor pleading for an abortion, even suggesting that this fifth pregnancy might have been the result of an affair with Francis Russell, brother of Bertrand, whom she met at Maude Stanley's salon and saw annually in London. She kept her pregnancy a secret from everyone except her husband and then in September she left Nassenheide for England.

Elizabeth returned home with her fifth child, the long-awaited heir, Henning Bernd von Arnim, in December of 1902, introducing the boy to the family by plonking him under the Christmas tree and claiming he had been dug up in a parsley patch. According to the Usborne biography, 'His mother was never to forgive him for intruding into her life and showed him little mercy', adding that Beatrix 'remembered that he was beaten every day "because he was not wanted" and that his sisters "were horrified"'. In the months after his birth, Usborne believes that Elizabeth fell into a deep depression, possibly for as long as two years, while she tried to cope with five children. However, this suggestion is difficult to reconcile with the fact that much of the writing of *The Adventures of Elizabeth in Rugen*, one of her funniest and most lighthearted books, was undertaken during this time and reviewers agreed that it was also among her happiest. In 1904 it was published to unanimously good reviews, with Cecily Sidgwick of *The Bookman*, finding it extremely useful as a practical travel guide but more importantly, added that the author 'makes her readers happy from the beginning to the end'.

Not only could Elizabeth *do* happiness in her everyday life – as her holiday amply demonstrates – she could *write* happiness and convey it to her readers. Her characters, often a version of herself (like every self-obsessed writer) experienced wondrous moments of ecstasy and joy, which were then vicariously experienced by the reader.

Since Elizabeth's time, the attainability of happiness has become the subject of countless contemporary books. 'How to Be Happy' tomes fill the self-help shelves of our bookshops, each one offering wise counsel. These books are similar, in my experience, to the admirable Christian sermons that preach goodness and morality, homilies that I listened to attentively for years, but from which I always came away being just as bad (or good) as I was before hearing them.

It has taken me most of my lifetime to realise that I cannot learn from lectures. Even though I make my living as a lecturer, like my father before me, I can only learn from concrete models, not abstract words. Which is why I eventually concluded that the way to be happy was to copy what happy people do rather than what happiness gurus say. But it's so rare to meet genuinely happy people that models are extremely difficult to come by. So much *talk* about happiness, so many books, so many theories, so many studies – and so few concrete examples of the real thing.

The difference between Elizabeth's books and the piles of contemporary volumes theorising about happiness is her extraordinary ability to *demonstrate* happiness in her novels, rather than just talk about it. In her happiest and most famous novel, *The Enchanted April*, set in sunny Southern Italy, the reader vicariously rejoices as she witnesses the transformation of four women – one young, beautiful and much sexually harassed, two trapped in frustrating marriages and the fourth a cranky old spinster – from discontent to serenity.

Readers are not expected to believe that the serenity is permanent but the novel does encourage a genuine faith in enchantment, if only for a single month. In fact, Elizabeth can be so convincing that I met a reader recently who had embarked on a holiday precisely with the intention of recreating von Arnim's enchanted April. I had to admit that the book had had exactly the same effect on me – although, unsurprisingly, I am yet to achieve the reality of a month's holiday in a castle overlooking the bay of Portofino. Nevertheless, my faith in the possibility remains and that's why I feel so indebted to this forgotten, quirky, antiquated author.

In later years, Elizabeth reminisced about her time at Nassenheide as possibly the happiest of her life. She had certainly found solace at Nassenheide and freedom to write but it was a remote and alienated solace, a condition of self-isolation that much of the world is now intimately acquainted with. She admits that after receiving visitors – 'rare calls' in her neck of the woods – she sometimes lapsed into depression.

> That is the worst of being bed enough and clothed enough and warmed enough and of having everything you can reasonably desire – on the least provocation you are made uncomfortable and unhappy by such abstract discomforts as being shut out from a nearer approach to your neighbour's soul; which is on the face of it foolish, the probability being that he hasn't got one.

Notwithstanding her self-admonishment, she continued to pine for a soul mate: 'I long more and more for a kindred spirit – it seems so greedy to have so much loveliness to oneself – but kindred spirits are so very, very rare; I might as well cry for the moon.'

Elizabeth never seriously considered our contemporary notion that a husband could be a kindred spirit; the two roles are assumed to be utterly incompatible. This is certainly true of my own experience of husbands. My kindred spirits have always been friends, rather than lovers. In fact, I am a little envious of Elizabeth's relationship with her spouse, despite the ructions, precisely because she appears to have no expectations of him to be her soul mate and is quite content with his absence much of the time. Even when he was home, she could retreat to the library, which he apparently rarely entered. A mostly absent husband and a personal library has always been my idea of bliss.

In 1904, as part of Elizabeth's recovery from bearing her fifth child, and presumably as a way to carve out time to write, a tutor by the name of Fräuleine Teppi Backe was employed for the older girls. Teppi took up residence at Nassenheide and quickly developed a love and devotion for her employer, eventually taking on the role of housekeeper, lady's companion and surrogate mother to Elizabeth's occasionally neglected children, all of whom wanted more attention from their fun-loving, charismatic mother than she could afford to give. Soon it was realised that these extra duties left Teppi little time for tutoring and the search for a replacement began.

Elizabeth's nephew, Sydney Waterlow, suggested a fellow student at Cambridge by the name of Edward Forster as a possible candidate for the job and the young graduate was duly engaged. On arrival at the train station late one evening after a long journey, he found there was nobody to meet him. Many years later, E.M. Forster reflected on his inauspicious arrival at Nassenheide:

> Never shall I forget it ...When I arrived there it was dark. We drew up in the middle of a farmyard. Heaps of manure, with water between them, could be seen in the light that fell from the carriage windows, but of the Countess von Arnim not a sign.

Later, in a letter to his mother, he wrote:

> My arrival here was beyond my wildest dreams ...We trod in puddles, there was no road ... Presently I hit a large building which had a light in the upper window. I found a bell in it and rang. A hound bayed inside ... I rang again, and at last a dishevelled boy, with no light, appeared.

The boy unlocked the door and asked what is was the stranger wanted. Forster answered: 'I want to live here.'

According to Forster, Elizabeth's first words were: 'How d'ye do, Mr. Forster. We confused you with the housemaid.' Later Elizabeth claimed that when she first met the newly engaged tutor she almost dismissed him immediately because he was wearing such an ugly tie. Forster, having read the famous *Elizabeth and her German Garden*, was a little in awe of his employer whom he considered to be 'a gifted authoress'. He later reported that the idyllic images invoked in the writer's first book did not reflect the reality he found.

> The German garden itself, about which Elizabeth had so amusingly written, did not make much impression. Later in the summer some flowers came into bloom, and there were endless lupins which the Count was drilling for agricultural purposes. But there was nothing of a show and Nassenheide appeared to be surrounded by paddocks and shrubberies.

Had Elizabeth exaggerated the exquisite beauty of her garden in Pomerania? Or did Forster find it difficult to appreciate an unconventional garden that was 'natural' rather than formal and ordered, as was still the norm in England? Perhaps this is evidence of her extraordinary talent to see beauty where others could not.

Soon after arriving Forster reported to his mother:

> I don't see much of E who is engaged on a book, but when I do see her she is most pleasant and amusing; and I think I shall like her very much. She is, as I rather expected, nicer than her books, and I don't feel in awe of her ...

Very soon the two writers struck up a rapport. Elizabeth invited Forster into her *Triebhaus*, a place where others were forbidden to enter. There she proudly showed him her new

Remington typewriter on which she was to compose more than a dozen novels. They shared a passion for Jane Austen and in the evenings Forster read from the novels aloud, 'the two of them allies against the dreadful philistinism all around them'. Elizabeth was also quick to recognise his literary ability. The young aspiring writer recorded in his diary a comment from his employer:

> My dear fellow – I don't know whether you are so supremely great or whether you are on my level, and that is why you seem so marvellous. You are now 26, and it's the first of many times I shall sit at the feet of my juniors.

Forster noted that after reading an essay of his, Elizabeth had 'implied that he was an extremely dark horse of genius'. Afterwards the younger writer reflected: 'Not only was she clever, but she had the power of making one accept her categories, and I wasted much time in wondering how dark I was.'

Together they discussed writing, including the particular difficulty of endings. Both realised that, although they shared an admiration of Austen, they could no longer end novels as she did. Forster wrote in his diary: 'artists now realise that marriage, the old full stop, is not an end at all'. As they developed their literary discussions, Forster and Elizabeth fell into so many heated intellectual arguments that the Count eventually banned the topic of writing and books at the dinner table.

Forster described Elizabeth as 'small and graceful, vivid and vivacious' but as he got to know her, he also came to understand that she was a 'capricious and a merciless tease'. She was clearly generous, as he admits that he was 'underworked', his teaching duties amounting to only an hour a day, which left him much time for writing. 'I had abundant leisure for my German and my writing and was most considerately treated if I asked for leave.'

It appears that Forster became much less a tutor and much more an intellectual companion for his employer. Elizabeth had at last found a kindred spirit. Later in his literary career Forster used his 'Pomeranian recollections' to write *Howards End*, whose central characters, the German-English Schlegel sisters, were possibly inspired by Elizabeth's daughters. The two remained firm friends and in 1959, eighteen years after Elizabeth's death, Forster delivered a broadcast for the BBC called 'Recollections of Nassenheide', expressing regret that von Arnim's books had become 'much neglected'.

Happiness Principle Number Six:
A Kindred Spirit

By 1905 Elizabeth had finally got back to her writing. This time it was a fairy tale of sorts, about a German princess running away from the conventions and strictures of royalty in search of a simple life in the English countryside. The story begins with

Princess Priscilla and her tutor, the noble-minded Fritzing, escaping the royal castle on bicycles. Eventually they settle in a small English village where the well-meaning Priscilla, through thoroughly good intentions, comically manages to upset the status quo of the entire community.

The comedy lies in one of Elizabeth's favourite themes: the clash between the concept of the ideal and the real – in this case, Priscilla's naïve vision of a simple life in a rural cottage clashes with the muddy, cold reality of uncomfortable exile. Priscilla clings to her faulty vision rather than relent to the concrete and very flawed actuality confronting her because she believes that physical realities are not important; she is only interested in nourishing her soul. In a sense, Elizabeth is satirising herself.

The Princess Priscilla's Fortnight gives the impression of a playful children's story and yet there is also much of the profound in this novel. Elizabeth enjoys making fun of the lofty, philosophical idealists who reach for the pure and the absolute while ignoring the daily mundane chores, such as keeping the body warm, clothed and fed – the dull necessities that are so often relegated to women.

Priscilla fails in her bid to live the simple life but the sternly ironic narrator still applauds her for having the courage to attempt to live according to her philosophy – for taking risks and for aiming, however foolishly, for the unattainable. The alternative is a dull predictable and safe steadiness with no highs and none of what Elizabeth refers to as the 'large hours'. The narrator ends with typical irony:

It is always better, I believe, to be cautious and careful, to husband your strength, to be deadly prudent and deadly dull. As you would poison, so you should avoid doing what the poet calls living too much in your large hours. The truly prudent never have large hours; nor should you, if you want to be comfortable. And you get your reward, I am told, in living longer; in having, that is, a few more of those years that cluster round the end, during which you are fed and carried and washed by persons who generally grumble.

This passage is the first evidence of what would become the major preoccupation in Elizabeth's final two novels – the problem of aging as a woman. At thirty-nine, Elizabeth already had a preference for larger and fewer hours rather than longer days that led to drawn-out finales, and in particular she did not want 'more of those years that cluster round the end'.

One of the reasons I have become so preoccupied with the notion of happiness is precisely because I am getting closer to those years that cluster round the end. My upbringing by three fierce social activists – my mother, my father and my sister – taught me that our main purpose was to 'make a difference'. My mother spent her life volunteering for the People For Nuclear Disarmament and the Women's International League for Peace and Freedom; my father wrote about the influence of corporate power to undermine democracy – work some now describe as prophetic – and my sister dedicated her life to investigative journalism. Their lives were purposeful and meaningful but not often happy. And the years that clustered around the end were remarkably unhappy. This was largely because to them, the thought of making happiness a priority would have seemed selfish. So they simply never got into the habit.

While it is rather late in life to be trying to detach from the 'making a difference' philosophy, which played the role of religion in my family, I have come to believe that being happy can also make a difference. One of the most truly happy people I have met was the comedian John Clarke – and his happiness really did make a difference, as evidenced by the nationwide grief at his sudden death. Mourners often commented on how much they would miss 'the sparkle in his eye' and one of the last things I heard him say was, 'Try to enjoy life – I do!'

For her next book, Elizabeth decided to return to a landscape more grounded in her immediate reality. For that, she concluded, she needed to undertake real-life research and advertised herself as an English governess. Employment was soon offered in the household of a professor in the nearby town of Jena. Assuming the name of Miss Armstrong, Elizabeth told her new employer that she was an English woman on vacation from her post at the von Arnim household and wished to improve her German. Her story was accepted without question.

Elizabeth's new situation was in a lower middle-class home and she was accommodated in an unheated attic room. Domestic tasks included shopping, carrying heavy bags up flights of stairs, and mending the family's clothes. The author's research trip was cut short, however, when the professor's son fell in love with her, yet more proof of how charismatic she was – and for some men, almost magnetic. This uninvited romance gave Elizabeth far more material than she had expected. As was her habit, she transformed the raw material of her experience into a work of comedy as well as philosophical reflection on how a woman can mould a life that on the surface seems meagre into something meaningful.

Fräulein Schmidt and Mr. Anstruther is an epistolary novel, set in the same small town where the author was briefly employed, and composed entirely of letters between a German professor's daughter, Rose-Marie Schmidt, and the visiting English student, Roger Anstruther, who has come to Germany to study the language with Rose-Marie's father. On the eve of his departure Roger proposes to Rose-Marie and she immediately falls into a state of romantic ecstasy. But on returning to England, Roger finds he has a better offer from a wealthy young woman and breaks off the engagement with the impoverished Rose-Marie. Their correspondence continues nevertheless and eventually Roger realises the folly of his decision, begs forgiveness, and re-offers his renewed love. Rose-Marie refuses, preferring to be poor and independent.

The entire book is a philosophical argument between Rose-Marie and her once-devoted lover. The topics are the usual: marriage, happiness, and the apparent impossibility of combining the two. An insight into Elizabeth's philosophy around anonymity is also disclosed in this novel, explaining, at least in part, her insistence on keeping her identity a secret.

Early in the narrative, as a result of reading a book about the lives of the great poets, the heroine is left painfully disappointed by the god-like men she has admired for so long. Devastated to find that Coleridge was a drug addict and Milton a deficient husband and father, she flings the book across the room, deciding that 'all present and future poets should wrap themselves sternly in an impenetrable veil of anonymity'. In other words, what appears as sublime on the page should not be traced back and compared to the reality of its earthly source. Heroes are best left at a safe distance.

Anonymity, for Elizabeth, was a spiritual principle. Whenever there is 'even one spark of the Divine' it is necessary to maintain 'the dignity of separation, of retirement, of mystery'. Of one of her favourite authors, Rose-Marie writes: 'I am glad Thoreau is dead. I love him far too much ever to want to see him; and how thankful I am he cannot see me.'

'Presumably I agreed with her,' wrote Elizabeth of Rose-Marie, 'was she not my mouthpiece? The trumpet through which, morning after morning, I so busily blew ...?'

Other views of Rose-Marie's which can presumably be attributed to the author mainly hinge on happiness, a devotion to 'the simple life' and living in the present. When Rose-Marie suffers from a life-threatening illness, she declines to reveal any details to the tortured Roger:

> You ask me to tell you more about my illness, but I am afraid I must refuse. I see no use in thinking of painful past things. They ought always to be forgotten as quickly as possible; if they are not, they have a trick of turning the present sour, and I cling to the present, to the one thing one really has, and like to make it as cheerful as possible – like to get, by industrious squeezing, every drop of honey out of it.

She instructs her former lover on how joy can be extracted from the most mundane aspects of everyday existence:

> I never tire of pondering and watching and wondering. The way in which eternal truths lurk along one's path ... sit among the stones, hang upon the bushes, come into one's room in the morning ... come out at night in heaven with the stars never leave us, touch us, press upon us, if we choose to open our eyes and look, and our ears and listen – how extraordinary it is. Can one be bored in a world so wonderful? ...You must forgive this exuberance. The sun has got into my veins and has turned everything golden.

As usual, Elizabeth is way ahead in her understanding and advocacy of living in the moment. The happy ending of the novel is not brought about by a traditional romantic reconciliation followed by a marriage, à la *Pride and Prejudice* — such an outcome, according to Rose-Marie, would be a 'supreme catastrophe'. Instead, as a committed spinster, she spends her many empty hours translating and re-writing her father's manuscript, a work that has been repeatedly rejected by German publishers. The story ends when her version is accepted by an English publisher and Rose-Marie becomes a successful author, albeit behind the mask of her father. In this way, she has achieved a sense of self-worth that marriage could not have offered.

This idea of living in the moment — opening our 'eyes and look, and our ears and listen' was also what Elizabeth practised regularly in her life. At the beginning of every entry in Elizabeth's journals — which were often cryptic and limited to just a few lines — Elizabeth always noted the weather:

> Lovely quiet, warm summer's day ...
> Lovely weather, hot and gorgeous ...
> Brilliant blue day ...
> Grey, cooler, & windy ...
> Sweet still morning ...

When I first came to read her diaries I thought this was just a habit. But now I think differently. I've come to believe that her daily observations are more like a prayer, an honouring of the most important aspect of any day — the elemental power of the weather to determine our moods, and so much more. Was she also a kind of seer in this respect too? Did she recognise, long before anyone else, that weather is really the most important force of all? The force that will determine whether we happily go on existing on earth or whether we self-destruct?

In a sense, for Elizabeth, the weather is the only thing that matters. She honoured the weather because she honoured and loved the physicality of the world – sunshine, snow, storms and wind, twilight, sunrise and sunset. Sprawling in the sun was one of her favourite pastimes, whether it was in the alpine fields of Switzerland, the bay of Portofino or even, perhaps, on the shores of Kirribilli. Maybe the simple act of yielding to weather, of seeking out the idle pleasure of lying in the sun, is one of our easiest and most available sources of enchantment and happiness.

Happiness Principle Number Seven:
🌱 *Sunlight*

As I wander down the unmapped paths that a biography inevitably sends the biographer, I am reminded of how often these pathways end up as pilgrimages. Throughout my travels in pursuit of Elizabeth, I remembered another woman writer who had similarly inspired me to make a pilgrimage many years ago, all the way from Sydney to south-west Spain.

In my early twenties, when I was trying to work out how to be a writer, I was desperate to find real-life examples of women who could provide me with a model for pursuing my vocation. But even in the 1980s, almost a hundred years after Elizabeth's first book was published, I was yet to meet – in real life – an independent woman writer. For years, I fumbled blindly along without a model, driven by instincts but with no real design or vision, knowing I had a vocation but not knowing what that was exactly. And then I discovered Saint Teresa of Ávila.

Teresa, like Elizabeth, was intelligent, sharp, witty and literary. Born in 1515, she came from a noble family and as a young woman, also like Elizabeth, after observing her mother's laborious and unhappy life, she decided she was not keen on marriage. In sixteenth century Spain the only alternative to matrimony was to take the veil, so even though Teresa didn't consider herself particularly pious, she entered a Carmelite convent in the ancient walled city of Ávila. There she was expecting to lead a quiet, disciplined existence among like-minded women in her Carmelite community but soon realised that the cloistered life closely reflected the society outside: nuns from well-off families had bigger cells and better meals, and even entertained lovers, while the poorer sisters were obliged to work hard to sustain the order. Teresa's sense of justice was incensed and she set out to reform the convent and eventually established her own breakaway order known as the Discalced, or Barefoot Carmelites, who took their commitment to poverty and simplicity seriously. It was to be a contemplative order, focused on prayer and meditation and for the benefit of her novices, she wrote three books: *The Way of Perfection, The Interior Castle* and *Autobiography* (later published as *The Life of St Teresa of Ávila By Herself*).

It strikes me that if Elizabeth had been born a few centuries earlier, it is possible that, like Teresa, she might have entered a convent, the cloister being the only place she would be assured of finding solitude, books, and time to write. Nassenheide, in an earlier incarnation, had been a convent and possibly retained a sense of devotion and contemplation.

Teresa and Elizabeth have other similarities: they were both huge personalities, tremendously hardworking, funny, candidly unconventional and with temperaments that were intense and rapturous. (Teresa is said to have levitated regularly while Elizabeth frequently experienced rapture.) Both were gifted writers and both served as examples to other women, demonstrating to their contemporaries that there were ways of being that were beyond the prescribed expectations.

My own peculiar need for a kind of feminism that incorporates an ecstasy-seeking religious sensibility with a literary aesthetic – a combination that I now realise is as difficult to own up to as it is to find – meant that it took me many years to unearth the right role models. And how mysterious to have discovered one in a remote corner of Prussia and the other in a sixteenth century Spanish town. But how blessed I feel now, albeit belatedly, to have found them.

Again and again, Elizabeth's books and letters return to this one topic of happiness and yet after months of re-reading her novels I was still wondering: *What was her secret?* And I began to ponder whether the key possibly lay in the very secrecy itself.

I thought back to the passage from her memoir that reflected on the 'most purely happy moment' of her life – the moment she received her very first publisher's acceptance letter. In that, I felt there was a clue. But why had this happiness been so pure? Surely, it wasn't just about having her literary talent recognised. If that were the case, she would have immediately broadcast the news. Instead, she kept it completely to herself. Perhaps her happiness was pure because it was all hers. Maybe the conscious decision *not* to share her happiness – in an act that many might describe as selfish – was precisely the source of its purity. Her happiness was enduring because, while ever it was unshared, it also remained undiluted, undissipated and unadulterated. And it was all those pure things because it was completely private.

I am now convinced that this experience of having an utterly private happy secret is central to Elizabeth's philosophy. As women we have been taught, indeed indoctrinated, into sharing everything. Unlike men, we share the very interior of our bodies with other humans-in-the-making and perhaps this leads us to believe that the entirety of our internal worlds should also be shared. The idea that a woman can only be happy if she is *part of* something else – part of a family, part of a couple – is such a cultural certainty that women inevitably end up believing we are essentially puzzles in search of our missing pieces. Elizabeth has a different view. Not only is a woman capable of being happy in the company of other women, she suggests – even more contentiously – a woman is capable of being happy all on her own. And this was, and perhaps still is, her most revolutionary idea of all.

🌿

Most reviewers of *Fräulein Schmidt and Mr. Anstruther* seemed to miss the fact that this was the first of Elizabeth's books that, while playful, was also seriously philosophical. Virginia Woolf was entertained by the descriptions of life in a small German town but found the novel 'does not lift more weighty matters successfully'. (Elizabeth, although a great admirer of Woolf's work, wrote later that humour was 'the one gift of the gods withheld' from that modernist writer.) There were, however, numerous positive reviews, including one in *The Evening News*, concluding that *Fräulein Schmidt and Mr. Anstruther* 'has an insight into life which makes the author ... one of the finest, if not the finest, of present day writers'. And the *Times Literary Supplement*, in their obituary of Elizabeth, referred to this novel as her greatest achievement.

In 1907, upon reading *Fräulein Schmidt and Mr. Anstruther*, a Cambridge undergraduate sent the author a fan letter. He was twenty-three and she was forty-one. Elizabeth responded to her young admirer with the following: 'If you want to pour out your woes to a person who thinks rather like Rose-Marie on the subject of young men's sorrows write me a line. Your obliged, amused and interested "Elizabeth". Thus began a long friendship with Hugh Walpole.

The devoted fan was invited to the Lyceum, Elizabeth's club in London. He later described Elizabeth as 'a small, rather pretty woman. Very outspoken and sharp.' She quickly offered Walpole the position of tutor at Nassenheide and soon he was following in the footsteps of Forster.

Once he had taken up his situation, Walpole found his employer, who had initially charmed him over afternoon tea, difficult to handle. He wrote to a friend:

> The Countess is a complete enigma. I don't see much of her but, when I do, she has three moods (1) Charming, like her books only more so (this does not appear often). (2) Ragging. Now she is unmerciful – attacks you on every side, goes at you until you are reduced to idiocy, and then drops you, limp. (3) Silence. This is the most terrible of all. She sits absolutely mute and if one tries to speak one gets snubbed.

'Ragging' was also the word E.M. Forster applied to Elizabeth, meaning a particularly savage form of teasing, a habit that one biographer refers to as a war on Walpole's innocence, and a practice that for the young tutor, occasionally reduced him to tears.

Nevertheless, the two writers developed a friendship that, although perhaps not of the kindred-spirit kind, lasted a lifetime. Unlike her admiration for her previous tutor's literary talent, Elizabeth didn't think highly of Walpole's later output. On writing to a friend, she quoted a particular sentence from a Walpole novel: 'To be a mother you have to have patience.'

'Fancy that,' she quipped to her correspondent, 'when I always thought it was a man you had to have.' Many years later, on reading Walpole's *Roman Fountain*, Elizabeth wrote in her diary: 'Poor Hugh. He so longs to be a great writer. I blushed for him, reading the stuff.'

Notwithstanding her ragging and criticism, Elizabeth remained fond of him and he of her. Walpole dedicated his 1915 novel *The Golden Scarecrow* to his former employer and at the age of seventy-one, Elizabeth responded to an affectionate letter from Walpole:

> Indeed I wish too that you were my godson, or any other sort of son. You are one of the few people I would like to be related to. And I believe you and I are two of the few people who are more often happy than unhappy, and say out loud that they are.

In the summer of 1907 Elizabeth began planning another escape that would again provide material for a novel. This time it was to be a caravan holiday around the south of England. She hired two caravans, drawn by a pair of huge dray horses, that set out from a soggy field in Surrey. The holiday party included Elizabeth's daughters Evi, Liebet and Beatrix as well as several former tutors, including E.M. Forster. The ladies slept in the vans and the young men in tents. Their holiday plans, however, were soon scuttled by the weather. It was to be the wettest August on record, and the horses struggled in the mud while the noise of rain hammering on the roof of the caravans caused sleepless nights. And yet constant rain still didn't dampen Elizabeth's spirits, as she 'walked up and down the entourage handing out biscuits and encouragement' never for a moment considering abandoning her expedition.

It was the kind of rustic holiday that utterly bemused Elizabeth's husband, and would have horrified the average member of the Prussian aristocracy, yet suited Elizabeth's pursuit of the Wordsworthian ideal of rural simplicity. All her life she had a Thoreau-like longing to live in a basic country cottage set in a field with a cow and vegetable patch. The sight of so many pretty English cottages during their travels through Kent convinced her that this was where she truly wanted to live and she made several offers to buy what appeared to be her ideal home.

Elizabeth's ideal home was always the next one. She moved house constantly, bought and sold almost on a whim, built three houses from scratch and lived in thirty-five houses over her lifetime. 'It is one of the things we have in common,' wrote H.G. Wells in his reflections on Elizabeth, 'that we are both haunted by a craving for a perfect house somewhere else.'

On returning from the caravanning holiday Elizabeth and her children travelled to London to join Henning at the Grosvenor Hotel, where according to Forster's journal, they enjoyed 'a great many baths and getting rid of the last of the dirt'. But Elizabeth found her husband ill and depressed. The summer had also been particularly wet in Pomerania, leading to the failure of crops and imminent ruin. If Elizabeth didn't bail him out Nassenheide would most surely end up in the hands of the receivers, who were expected to arrive any day.

By this time, the writer had been supporting the estate for years but financial solvency depended on her continuing to produce best-sellers. She had no private or inherited income of her own. It appears that the couple resigned themselves, after a tearful evening, to the loss of their beloved Nassenheide. This decision led to another major source of disagreement. Now that losing Nassenheide was a foregone conclusion, the family had to decide where to live; Henning wanted to stay in Prussia while Elizabeth insisted they move to England. The family returned to Pomerania without any consensus. Once at home in Nassenheide, her daughter Evi wrote in her diary about the continuing disharmony: 'There is really a very small amount of happiness on this earth and what is so bad, it is easily dispelled.' She blamed the unhappiness on her parents' differing upbringings and nationalities.

P. on one side brought up to despise all females and regarding them as if they belonged to a class entirely inferior in every way. Dear M. on the other side, witty, clever and altogether contrary to the accustomed German female ... it is the natural German thing; but how dreadful; the man is all, the woman nothing.

Clearly it was infuriating for Elizabeth that she was considered nothing when it was on the back of her labour and literary output that the whole family depended. Adding to her discontent was a daily personal habit of Henning's that had suddenly worsened; her husband had progressed from the practice of sucking water from his finger bowl to rinse his false teeth to the habit of keeping everyone at the dinner table waiting while he removed his dentures and washed them out. Elizabeth later told Wells that this had been 'the last straw' – soon after they would live separate lives, he in Prussia and she in England.

It was snowing in the spring of 1909 when the removalist vans arrived at Nassenheide in the fading evening light. They were ordered to remove everything as quietly as possible because Elizabeth was in fear that the creditors might turn up at any moment and seize her possessions. Henning stayed behind to negotiate the sale.

The family's first home in England was Blue Hayes at Broadclyst, near Exeter. At first, it appeared to be the perfect house – with a walled garden, tennis court, orchard and a garden studio as a writing retreat. But the children found it difficult to adjust. Elizabeth's son, Henning Bernd, spoke no English and was bullied at school. The children barely saw their mother because she was so busy trying to earn a living and responding to invitations from the locals who had become aware that the famous author was living among them. Added to this was a resentment building among her children who felt they were being forced to be English. It was during this time the problems with Felicitas, her second-youngest child, became exacerbated.

Throughout this difficult period of readjustment Elizabeth had no help from her husband. He only added to her worries by writing to say he was lonely and demanding that some of the children should return to Pomerania. When nobody came, Henning travelled to England and according to Evi's journal there were many days of bitter disagreements that produced 'lots of sulphur'. Despite her emotional and financial burden – at the age of forty-two, Elizabeth was now the sole provider for the family – in her letters she refused to reveal any sense of vulnerability and would never, under any circumstances, have considered herself a victim.

The narrator of *The Caravaners*, the novel inspired by Elizabeth's summer holiday in the south of England, is a pompous Prussian officer, Baron Otto von Ottringe. Biographer Usborne describes Otto as 'self-centred, a snob and the original male chauvinist pig, a superb caricature of the typical Prussian bourgeois'. Much of his character, it has been assumed, was based on the Count. Usborne goes on to comment: 'Clearly this was not a book designed to promote peace in the von Arnim household.'

Fortunately for the family, *The Caravaners*, published in November 1909, sold well. Readers enjoyed the satire of the German temperament, something similar to Jerome K. Jerome's 1900 novel, *Three Men on the Bummel*, about cycling through Germany. In the wake of the publication, caravanning suddenly became a fashionable activity for feminists and 'for several years landowners had to cope with a small army of literary females and their friends' haranguing the locals about women's right to vote.

Only a year after moving into Blue Hayes, Elizabeth decided to sell. Her first English home had been an unhappy one, despite her having created yet another magnificent garden. The children were sent to various boarding schools while Elizabeth moved into a flat in Whitehall. She gathered the family again for one last dismal Christmas at Nassenheide and then stayed on after the children had returned to school, ostensibly to accompany her ill husband who was invisible except at meals. She wrote to Liebet that she spent 'exciting days in my *Treibhaus* tidying and cleaning up my soul which has got into a great confusion and muddle lately'. Once she had finished her tidying, she said, she planned to return to England.

Nassenheide was finally sold in 1910 and Henning's doctor recommended that he go to a sanatorium. Elizabeth dutifully sat with her husband for several weeks, despite his irritable state, and when he appeared to improve slightly, she returned to London for the opening of her play *Priscilla Runs Away*, an adaptation of her novel, written with the assistance of J.M. Barrie and produced for the Theatre Royal Haymarket by Irish playwright Herbert Trench. There she was joined by her three eldest daughters who were instantly recognised as the April, May and June babies who had so enchanted her readers. After repeated rounds of applause, the playwright still refused to appear before the audience so bouquets were presented to the children in her stead.

Priscilla Runs Away was a West End hit, both a financial and critical success. Feeling confident again, as well as solvent, Elizabeth travelled to Kissengen, where Henning had been moved to a more suitable sanatorium, possibly a kind of hospice. Immediately she realised how much he had worsened and wired the children to come. Henning died two days after their arrival, on 20 August 1910.

🌿

After her husband's death, Elizabeth felt liberated. No longer part of the oppressive Prussian aristocracy or burdened by the heavy duties of being a German wife, she was at last free to become the full-time professional writer she had always longed to be. The children were farmed out – the two eldest were sent to Cambridge, Beatrix was sent to Berlin, while the two youngest returned to boarding schools.

Following Henning's funeral and the accompanying formalities, Elizabeth felt she needed to recover her 'soul' and travelled to Switzerland, having set her sights on the Swiss mountains as a possible location for her next home. Later she was to write that she was behaving 'altogether as persons do behave who have lately, for the first time in their lives, become completely free, and responsible to no authority of any kind'. She recounts recklessly buying picturesque sites in the alps, 'which turned out to be impossible because, except beauty, they had nothing – no roads, no water, none of what must be there if houses are to be built'. In other words, she had turned into a moderately wealthy, exceedingly merry widow.

While searching for a site for her new home, in late 1910 Elizabeth took up residence in Hotel Victoria, overlooking Lake Geneva. There she found a letter waiting for her from H.G. Wells. She responded:

> Dear Mr H.G.,
> I've escaped from Berlin and am on my way to Sierre, and feel born again.

She goes on to invite him to her chalet still under construction and signs the letter 'Yours sincerely, Elizabeth Arnim'.

It is from this time, in her period of newfound freedom and re-birth, that Elizabeth began to openly identify with the persona of her pen-name. In 1907, her first letter to Wells – she had been writing to him as a fan – was signed 'Mary Arnim'. Now, three years later and writing as a friend, she was no longer burdened by the reputation of a woman married into the extremely conservative German aristocracy; she could come out from behind the shield of anonymity, which by then was more like a thin veil, her identity having become an open secret.

Before returning to London she read an advance copy of Wells's controversial *The New Machiavelli* about an adulterous affair based on his relationship with Amber Reeves. From the Hotel Château Bellevue in Sierre, Elizabeth wrote again:

Dear Mr Wells,

You must forgive me for bothering you with my extreme joy over your wonderful Machiavelli – never did a man understand things as you do. The others only guess and theorize – you know and the poetry of it, and the aching desolating truth! What one longs to read, written by you, is the study of the afterwards – what happened to them as the dreadful ordinary years passed with all their days full of getting up, and walking and having meals, and going to bed, and no friends anywhere, and just their two selves. Is anyone strong enough in love and fine thinking to stand the effect of all the little hours?

Yours ever gratefully
Elizabeth von Arnim.

'The afterwards' she was referring to was in relation to the adulterous couple in *The New Machiavelli* who are essentially exiled from British society. The concerns expressed in Elizabeth's letter are reminiscent of her conversations with E.M. Forster about the difficulty of endings in the modern era, of the impossibility of 'Happily Ever After', of the huge chasm between the 'little' and 'large' hours, as well as the great courage it takes to live large, as Elizabeth dared to do. But there is also something bold and flirtatious in her question, almost daring Wells to rise to the occasion and say, 'Yes! I can be the one strong enough in love! I can show you how!'

And according to some versions of their shared history, he did.

H.G. Wells and Elizabeth von Arnim went on to enjoy a deep lifelong friendship but whether it was platonic or a passionate love affair is still a topic for debate. Wells's autobiography claims they were lovers and that their lovemaking was so vigorous that they caused beds to break in more than one hotel during their extensive travels together. Elizabeth's daughter's account of her mother insists that the relationship was chaste, much to Wells's frustration. Von Arnim biographer Jennifer Walker strenuously rejects the idea that H.G. was a lover, believing that Elizabeth was possibly 'the one woman to refuse him'. But in the very same biography a photo is included that appears so intimate it seems impossible to believe their relationship wasn't physical. Like so much about this inscrutable author, we will never know for certain one way or the other.

Throughout 1912 and 1913 H.G. Wells and Elizabeth were increasingly seen together. Her diary records meeting up with 'G', as she called Wells, on 30 January 1912, 'to tea and walk on Embankment', followed by many other lunches and outings. Then in March there was a falling out, followed by an uncomfortable meeting, recorded by Elizabeth as 'Lunched with G. New Gallery – disastrous'. This pattern seemed to continue while Elizabeth travelled between London and Switzerland, where she was busy building her dream home, a hotel-sized chalet in one of the most stunning areas of the alps, the mountain slopes above Rhone Valley in the Canton du Valais, near Randogne sur Sierre. She engaged an architect, instructing that she wanted sixteen rooms on the upper two storeys while the ground floor would be dedicated to relaxation, meditation and dining. Of her seven toilets, she would later comment: 'Whenever I feel depressed and lonely I remember all my lavatories and am comforted.'

Wells claims that while building the Chalet Soleil, Elizabeth arranged to install a secret door behind a wardrobe that moved on well-oiled castors. In that way the lovers could say a platonic 'good night' to each other and maintain what he described as 'nocturnal decorum'. Elizabeth also arranged to have another small house constructed to one side of the main chalet, known as the Little Chalet, where she could write in solitude, away from her constant guests. It was here that many of her books were composed.

On several occasions Wells accompanied Elizabeth on her trips to Montana and it was while walking the Swiss mountains that he claims they made love 'on sun-flecked heaps of pine-needles under the straight trees' after picnicking on bread, ham and beer. In his book *H.G. Wells in Love: Postscript to an Experiment in Autobiography*, he gives details:

One day we found in a copy of *The Times* we had brought with us, a letter from Mrs Humphrey Ward denouncing the moral tone of the younger generation, and, having read it aloud, we decided we had to do something about it. So we stripped ourselves under the trees as though there was no one in the world but ourselves, and made love all over Mrs Humphrey Ward.

He alleges that afterwards they lit a match and burned the offending article.

Wells's memoir includes a chapter devoted to his relationship with Elizabeth entitled 'The Episode of Little E'. In it, he claims that their friendship blossomed into an affair when he went to Cotchet Farm near Haslemere, not far from where Elizabeth was staying with her sister, Charlotte. (In 1911, she had spent Christmas in that area.)

Wells writes that:

When she heard talk of my scandalous life ... it seemed to her that I was eminently fitted to correct a certain deficiency of her own ... We liked each other; we laughed together; we made love very brightly, but I cannot imagine a relationship more free from passion than ours.

According to Wells's account, they quickly became lovers. He described her as a woman who 'mingled adventurousness with extreme conventionality in a very piquant manner'. He also claims that she had found sex with her husband a 'serious and disagreeable business', partly because he 'never smelt quite right' but that she 'was aware that it might be far less onerous'.

It is possible, of course, that Wells made all this up. The chapter in his memoir about Elizabeth is full of inaccuracies. Wells asserts that Elizabeth was Irish, that her brother was a Dublin physician and that she had eloped with her first husband and later left him. 'When she became my mistress,' writes

Wells, 'he was already dead and she was a widow'; a statement that is at least two-thirds correct – Henning's deadness and Elizabeth's widowhood. What remains uncertain, at least in the eyes of two of von Arnim's biographers, is her role as mistress.

In November 1912, Elizabeth was planning to leave London for her newly constructed Chalet Soleil. On the eve of her departure, she recorded a meeting with Wells thus: 'Had tea outside in wonderful grey and mauve and quiet and gloom, then sat by Serpentine watching lights – he took me home – talk and farewell.'

The impression is that this was supposed to be a final farewell – not just a temporary goodbye. But then Wells later phoned to say he would see her off at Victoria Station, claiming he wanted to go with her to Switzerland. Elizabeth records, however, that 'he did not want to enough. Saw, in this way, the last of G.' On arriving at the chalet she 'wrote to G. bowing myself out. Alas for the end of what was going to be so lovely.'

The expression 'bowing myself out' implies a retreat from a relationship that included more than a couple of people. The timing of Elizabeth's decision coincided with Wells taking up with the much younger writer and critic Rebecca West – leaving the incorrigible philanderer with three intimate relationships to manage: his wife Jane, Elizabeth and Rebecca. Despite Elizabeth's daughter's claim that her mother's relationship with Wells was platonic, it is a view that seems inconsistent with the circumstances, as well as the diaries.

Wells responded to Elizabeth's break-off message with a stream of reproachful letters, followed by telegrams. When

Wells didn't get the response he wanted, he then turned up at the chalet in person to seek a reunion and 'horrid talks' ensued, leading to a heated departure on 2 December. Elizabeth was so distraught that her dear friend Teppi observed later that she had never seen her mistress brought to such a state. This fact alone suggests strongly that their relationship went further than friendship.

'Suitors are, after all, a strain,' Elizabeth wrote much later in her memoir.

Certainly, in my experience, suitors have always come with too much strain to make the effort worthwhile. My long and undistinguished line of boyfriends, lovers and husbands began in high school with tanned surfers, after which I took up with an olive-skinned Italian hippy, followed by an Irish folk guitarist, a Mexican coffee farmer, a Belfast blacksmith, an Australian tradie, an English editor, a Caribbean novelist, and finally, a much younger, dangerously handsome Irishman, which led to a stormy decade of sex and alcohol, ending in a messy separation and an expensive financial settlement. By then, the strain had reached catastrophic proportions.

Three years after the Irishman had vanished and I was sure the suitors had finally come to an end, a friend almost twenty years my junior emailed me with a semi-formal and very flattering written proposal. In it he argued how much we had in common and that our romantic liaison (if I chose to accept it) would be bound to succeed, given the strong foundation of our decades-long friendship.

I agreed with much of what he proposed; his contribution to my life would have made every aspect of it much easier and more pleasant. I would have company instead of living alone; I would have a piano duet partner; a companion with whom I could eat, drink and go to the opera, not to mention someone to help out with household bills. So why did it take me less than two hours to refuse? Because suitors are, after all, a strain. And having had a taste of the suitorless lifestyle, the prospect of going back required a faith in romantic love I no longer possess.

'Dislike love,' noted Elizabeth in her diary, 'and loathe scenes.'

Amen.

In the new year of 1913 Elizabeth von Arnim was determined to put her stormy love life behind her and focus on her writing, recording in late January, 'Began my book'. This referred to the novel many believe to be her most accomplished, *The Pastor's Wife*. In less than a month however, her persistent suitor intervened, arriving at the chalet again at the end of February, which immediately led to their usual pattern of quarrelling followed by reconciling. The diary gives no specifics about what all these emotional scenes were about. If she had been writing about a warring couple in one of her novels, we would know the exact nature of their conflict and the precise words and accusations but Elizabeth was too private for that. However, there have been some guesses by biographers as to the nature of these continuous fights:

a) he wanting more than friendship and she refusing to get physical;
b) she wanting an offer of marriage and he not wanting to leave his wife; and/or
c) his affair with Rebecca West.

In March Elizabeth recorded: 'G. & I left for London – dined at Sierre – he went by 8.18, I by 9.25.' Deliberately travelling by different trains seems to indicate that they couldn't be seen arriving in London together, further confirming the theory that they were a couple trying to keep their relationship secret. Nevertheless, they continued to meet regularly, causing scandal and gossip, made worse, no doubt, when they both took apartments in St James' Court. Wells also had a key to Elizabeth's apartment, a detail that again suggests intimacy rather than friendship.

In May of 1913, after a tour of Europe accompanied by a bad-tempered Wells, Elizabeth recorded that she had had 'more than enough' and left for the chalet, noting on arrival that it was 'Lovely to be free again'. The very next day she was back at work on *The Pastor's Wife*, using her recent experience of an unhappy European holiday as material for her new book.

Within a month, Wells was back at the chalet and Elizabeth's diary records 'things all honey again'. In May she records that she and H.G. walked to Lens, a village nearby, and 'got restored to peace'. Then on 5 November, there was another blow-up and Elizabeth records:

> G's departure out of my Life! Thank God – Restored to Freedom … His last remark as he left the chalet and I bade him farewell was, 'It's all because I'm so <u>common</u>'.

Wells's version of why the relationship broke down is as follows:

> … it came to an end because perhaps of the same freakish quality that had begun it … She wanted to get more out of me than the fun and fellowship I gave her. She wanted us to feel the keen edge of life together – in spite of the fact that we had both resolved it should never cut us … More and more did she resent the fact that I kept our love light-hearted … she would sit up on the mountain turf in the sunlight scolding me and telling me the Whole Duty of a Lover, as she now conceived it … She was taking the fun out of our relationship and it was the fun that held us together.

He goes on to claim that Elizabeth had begun to be demanding: 'Had I ever wept about her or trembled to come near her? *Real* lovers did. Would I even interrupt my work for her? "Not a bit of it," I said, "for you or anyone." '

Such comments would have been very uncharacteristic. Elizabeth, as a wife, housekeeper and mother of five children, understood far more keenly than Wells the need of privacy and solitude for a writer, and she also hated being interrupted. On the other hand, her feelings towards Wells were clearly intense and she was probably just as capable of irrationality and contradiction as any other disappointed lover.

The part of Wells's account of the relationship that does ring true is the story of their final break-up. 'We severed ourselves in a talk in her London drawing-room,' he writes.

'It was your fault,' she said, 'You were only half a lover.'
'It was your fault,' said Wells. 'You didn't really love' ...
'Only half a lover,' she sang. 'Only half a lover.'

This may have been the end of their romance but it did not spell the end of their relationship. Afterwards, they were reunited as friends and remained so for life. Wells reports that: 'We had always liked each other's humour and, now that there was no pretence of romantic love or urgent desire to distort our behaviour, we could laugh freely.' In fact, in later life they took up residence in the same village in the south of France, and often enjoyed each other's company.

Anthony West, Wells's son by Rebecca West, interpreted his father's affair with Elizabeth as follows: 'My impression is that his inability to deliver a major emotional response in a love affair was looked on as a positive asset ... and that his quickness and lightness were just what she wanted.'

On reflection later, Wells described Elizabeth as 'comic and malicious and unendurable', telling Frank Swinnerton that, 'When you've had her for five days you want to bang her head through the wall.' Elizabeth's comment about Wells to Swinnerton was that he was 'a coarse little man' and her diary sums him up as follows: 'H is a genius – with two enormous feet of clay. Also clay in other parts of him – the clay of smallness, malice, spite, etc – ever wanting distinction.'

Typical writers, both Elizabeth and Wells used their relationship as material for fiction: *The Pastor's Wife* features the self-indulgent artist who beguiles and betrays the innocent heroine, while Wells's 1913 novel, *The Passionate Friends*, paints a prominent character, Lady Mary Justin, as follows:

> ... fair, very slightly reddish hair – it was warm like Australian gold ... and her mouth always smiled faintly ... with her eyes a little darkened, mocking me. It was all of these things and none of these things that made me hers, as I have never been any other person's ... Always we were equals, or if anything she was the better of us two ... Mary was not only naturally far more quick-minded, more swiftly understanding than I, but more widely educated ... I could not speak and read and think French and German as she could.

These are all attributes that could be applied to Elizabeth and suggests that she might have told Wells about her Australian origins. The book is mysteriously dedicated to L.E.N.S., which could mean both Little E and the village of Lens, a favourite hiking destination for the couple, and possibly – in my view, probably – the location of their lovemaking on sun-flecked pine needles.

With Henning, H.G. Wells and the children out of the way, Elizabeth finally had the opportunity to truly follow her vocation. *Princess Priscilla Runs Away*, the theatrical adaptation of her novel, had brought new audiences and increased fame and wealth, which meant she at last had the time and resources to devote herself to writing full-time. It is of note that the manuscript she finished at this time was very probably the one that she had started many years earlier in Berlin, in the early days of her marriage, and referred to in her diary as 'FW'. There are so many similarities between the marriage in *The Pastor's Wife* and her own with Henning that it is easy to believe she had been storing up this story, just waiting for her husband to die, in order to write what many believe to be her finest work.

Like Henning, the German husband in *The Pastor's Wife*, Robert Dremmel, is an agriculturalist obsessed with improving soils and strains of potato tubers. As the biographer Usborne notes of Henning: 'He stood at his tall desk night after night, burning the midnight oil in his attempts to produce a strain of potato on his farm that would make money in his doomed quest to salvage the estate.'

Also like Henning, the pastor's attitude towards his wife changes dramatically after marriage. Early in the novel, Dremmel reflects:

> He was glad he had been able to be so thoroughly in love. He was glad he had so promptly applied the remedy of marriage. His affection for his wife was quite satisfactory: it was calm, it was deep, it interfered with nothing. She held the honourable position he had always, even at his most enamoured moment, known she would ultimately fill, the position next best in his life after the fertilizers.

Ingeborg, the heroine of the novel, is continually pregnant, similar to Elizabeth during the first years of her marriage. 'It was the absence of pauses that beat her. She came to be, as the German phrase put it, in a continual condition of being blest.'

Eventually, the pastor's wife can bear it no longer and decides to beg her husband for a reprieve, as much for his potential happiness as hers.

> 'Don't you think this persistent parenthood might end now?'
>
> He stared at her in utter amazement . . .
>
> 'Anyhow I can't go on,' she cried, twisting her fingers about in an agony. 'There's so little of me to go on with. I'm getting stupider every day. I've got no brains left. I've got no anything.'

And then Ingeborg asks the question so central to Elizabeth's novels:

> 'Oh, Robert,' she appealed, 'it isn't as though it made you
> really happier – you don't really particularly notice the
> children when they're there – it isn't as though it made
> anybody really happier – and – and – I'm dreadfully
> sorry, but I've done.'

Robert has no sympathy and is 'deeply offended', 'his manhood outraged'.

Ingeborg goes to the local doctor to plead her case for leading a chaste life. In the waiting room, she unexpectedly meets her husband, who has also come to plead his case for a compliant and dutiful wife, hoping the doctor might help to 'bring her to reason', because for Herr Dremmel, 'the business of bringing a woman to reason had always seemed to him quite the most extravagant way of wasting good time.'

In the waiting room he says to his wife:

> 'Why have you come? ...You do not look ill. You were
> not ill this morning.'
> 'It's – psychological,' murmured Ingeborg unnerved ...

Ingeborg's husband doesn't understand the meaning of the word, let alone the psychological damage his wife is suffering or her longing to be something more than a housekeeper and a continual bearer of infants.

Later in the novel, when Ingeborg meets Edward Ingram, the artist (based on Wells), Edward asks the pastor's wife how she spends her time. 'First I cook and then I – don't cook.' And then she reveals her feelings about her status:

'I'm a wife. I'm a mother. I'm everything now except a mother-in-law and a grandmother. That's all there's left to be. I think they're rather dull things both of them.'

Unsurprisingly, *The Pastor's Wife* also develops into a story of escape. Ingeborg escapes her drab existence in the little village of Kokensee when Ingram convinces her to travel with him so he can paint her portrait 'in the right light' – the right light being in Italy. Ingeborg accepts his invitation – innocent of his intent – leaving a letter for her husband on his desk. The couple's tour around Italy together however, very possibly like Elizabeth's tours with Wells, is not conducive of happiness. Ingram is frustrated by her naïvety, her implausible gullibility, and also by her enchantment with Italy, rather than with him.

He was exasperated. This being with her among the hills and lakes of Italy that he had thought of as going to be the sweetest time he had known was sheer exasperation; for even in the evenings when he was in love with her ... he was irritably in love, and hardly knew whether it would give him more satisfaction to shake her or to kiss her. And annoying and perplexing as her untroubled conscience was it was yet not so annoying and perplexing as her wild joy in Italy … Who would have supposed that she would … take the background he had so carefully chosen for his lovemaking … and adore it beyond reason, and that he himself would turn into the background, incredible as it seemed, into just the background of his own background?

Ingeborg continues to believe Ingram's professed motive for taking her to Italy is genuine, and is unnerved by his talk of love. 'You're what I've been looking for in women all my life,' Ingram tells her, in words perhaps similar to those used by Wells.

'You're the dream come true. I've only tried to love before. And now you've come, and made me love, which we all dream of doing, and given me love, which we all dream of getting—'

Her pleasure became tingled with a faint uneasiness, for she wouldn't have thought, left to herself, that she had been giving him love. Pastor's wives didn't give love except to their pastors.

When Ingeborg remains stubbornly oblivious of the artist's real intentions, the frustrated lover announces bluntly that, having run away with him, she cannot return to her husband.

'Why do you tell me I can't go back, I can't go home?'
'They wouldn't have you …'

'They wouldn't have me? Who wouldn't? There isn't a
they. I've only got Robert—'

'He wouldn't ... And Kokensee wouldn't and
couldn't ... And Germany ... wouldn't and couldn't.
The whole world gives you to me. You're my mate now
for ever.'

The chapter ends:

'So that,' she heard herself saying in a funny clear voice,
'there's only God?'

'How, only God?' he asked, looking up at her.

'Only God left who wouldn't call it adultery?'

Ingeborg bravely decides to escape once more and returns to
her village, full of dread and expecting she will be duly and
harshly punished. But what awaits her is even worse. Since his
wife has withdrawn sexual favours, Dremmel has completely
lost interest in her, so much so that he hasn't even bothered to
open the letter she left on his desk confessing her unwitting
elopement. The last line of the novel reads like a resounding
thud: 'He had forgotten Ingeborg.'

Indifference, the reader understands, is the most painful
punishment of all.

In the afterword of the Virago edition of *The Pastor's Wife*, Lisa
St Aubin de Teran states unequivocally that it is von Arnim's

best novel, providing 'both a synthesis and an explosion of much that had come to a head with Henning's death'.

Contemporary reviews were also glowing. *The Observer* stated that: 'We never miss the consciousness of that reserved strength which is the backbone of the greatest satire.' *The Spectator* described it as 'brilliantly written' and interpreted a deeper message in the book – a warning to England about Germany's intentions:

> It may be useful not to forget that the destruction of England is the ultimate object of the whole people of Germany, military and intellectual, and that this object will be pursued with the enthusiasm and determination shown by Robert Dremmel.

Von Arnim's oeuvre had, deliberately or otherwise, become part of the genre of 'anti-invasion literature'.

Over the years, the Chalet Soleil became established as a place much visited by friends and relatives, a venue for house parties, theatre pieces, poetry recitals, games, philosophical debates, love affairs, witty banter, hilarity and intrigue. An invitation to Elizabeth's summer house was also an invitation into the intellectual and artistic elite. After a time, however, according to her daughter Liebet, the high spirits inspired by the mountain air also underlined the hostess's sense of 'apartness'. Surrounded by friends, admirers, fans and suitors perhaps she still felt, at some level, lonely, as she no longer had an intimate mate of any serious commitment. What the writer didn't know was that this creeping sense of loneliness would lead to the advances of yet another suitor.

On a snowy December afternoon in 1913, a mere three weeks after the final break-up with H.G. Wells, a tall elegant man by the name of Francis Russell, the brother of the famous philosopher, arrived somewhat unexpectedly at the Chalet Soleil. 'He hadn't been invited, but, on some pretext which I afterwards perceived to have been thin, just came.' Many years later, Elizabeth recorded his arrival as unlike the other guests she was accustomed to welcoming:

> ... this one was different; for this one, climbing slowly
> up the ice-covered path to my front door ... wasn't so
> much another guest as Doom. And from one's doom
> there is no escape.

Elizabeth von Arnim was determined, hardworking, outspoken, intelligent, independent and with no financial need of a husband. Yet with Francis Russell, from the moment he appeared at her door, she found herself 'already sunk in acquiescence'.

'But of course you must stay,' she announced to her guest, ignoring her 'sinking feeling' because she was 'filled with a highly handicapping sense of inevitability, of being pre-destined'.

Many years later, while writing her mock autobiography, *All the Dogs of My Life*, she reflected:

> I can't account for my behaviour. I had never before felt any desire to serve, to obey, to stand with bowed head and hands folded, to be, as it were, the handmaid of the lord. But from the first I was meek and pliable ...

Neither could her friends and family understand how she so rapidly transformed from a spirited, rebellious, 'devilish' character into a passive servant. When Russell left a fortnight later Elizabeth made some feeble attempts to resist his overtures but her suitor had already started proceedings to divorce his wife and his letters were full of adolescent-style declarations of his 'volcanic, bursting flow of red hot love'.

> Because you see you have the soul I have always sought, the thing that comes through me like light through a stained glass window, so that I am lit, so that my heart is all sweet fire. I love other people, I love everyone, because I love you. I feel I can do sweet gorgeous things, I set out to make people happy, because of the love of you shining in my heart ...

> You sweet wise thing; you tender thing, you little Artist, you delicate worshipful soul, you strong sturdy friend of my Heart, my sister, my mother, my love, my undeserved, unmerited fate, my pride, my treasure of

life, burning like a little flame in the heart . . .

You are so bright, so alive, so healthy, so sweet, and in your dear innermost so tender. You beautiful little thing, you dear beautiful little thing! I love you from the top of your hair to the smallest of your toe-tips.

These are just a few of the quotations extracted by Elizabeth from Francis's voluminous love letters. At this time, Elizabeth was overseeing the incineration of her papers in order to prevent her secrets being revealed by hungry biographers. Rather than extinguishing all that ardour forever, she preferred to reproduce, in barely legible handwriting, selected portions of Russell's abundant epistles onto the back of draft pages of *The Pastor's Wife*. In a note at the end of the seven pages of tightly transcribed quotations, she states: 'These are bits of some love letters written to me once. But it seemed sad to save nothing. So these bits were extracted before the holocaust.'

If these expressions of love were difficult to destroy when the relationship was well and truly over, how much harder to resist when they were freshly written in early 1914? After her trials with Henning and H.G., one might think she would take a break from men. But for how long can anyone – man or woman – refuse to accept what appears to be a genuine offer of deep and enduring love? Which, from all appearances, so closely resembled a genuine offer of deep and enduring happiness?

H.G. Wells believed that Elizabeth's submission to Francis Russell may have had a practical element: 'I do not know how far things went between Russell and Little e before the war, but the catastrophe of Aug 1914 made it highly desirable that she should recover British nationality.'

As well as other advantages, recovering her British citizenship would save the author's belongings in England from the possibility of confiscation as alien property. Possibly the biggest advantage of considering marriage to Russell was the benefit of changing her name; von Arnim would have been a conspicuous and unpopular surname in England at the time. And of course, there was the added attraction of the title: she would become Lady Russell.

Elizabeth's uncharacteristic submission to Francis Russell may also have been influenced by what would now be called the rebound factor. She had only very recently broken with H.G. Wells. Sexual or not, her relationship with 'G' had been intensely emotional and their break-up at the end of 1913 caused great pain on both sides. Falling for Francis may have seemed like a way to recover, not only her Britishness, but also her sense of self.

Biographer Karen Usborne claims that after Henning died, Elizabeth's relationship with her children went from bad to worse and implies that their mother was neglectful. It is clear that, once widowed, the author was much occupied with lovers as well as with her work. Penelope Mortimer, in the introduction to the Virago edition of *The Adventures of Elizabeth in Rugen*, refers to a serious and long-term estrangement between Elizabeth and her children. Liebet, the daughter with whom she remained closest, wrote a biography of her mother that provides only one guarded clue to the family dynamics:

> Living up to her expectations was hardly relaxing, and some of the children grew up to feel that it entailed too great a sacrifice of their own wishes and, indeed, individualities. A marked difference of opinion on this point exists among them to this day.

If Elizabeth were a male writer, I wonder if a biographer might consider this alleged detachment from children worth a mention. In the tradition of 'The Great Man', it would be taken for granted that genius must be served, no matter the consequences, and that detaching from children was a necessity in order to complete great works. But for a woman writer, relationships with her children will inevitably be scrutinised and often to her detriment. Indeed, a biographical study of a woman artist will often be viewed primarily through the lens of her relationships with family, husbands and lovers rather than through the creative work itself. Wise is the woman writer who, like Elizabeth, chooses carefully which documents will remain after her death and which will be burned.

By January 1914, Elizabeth is deeply in love again, her journal recording: 'Got a wonderful letter from Francis. Wondered if it wouldn't shine through me visibly and give me away.' A week later she notes: 'Brilliant day. Meant to work but thought of F. & happiness instead.' In February Francis visited the chalet again and Elizabeth records: 'Francis & I all day sitting in sun.' And then on 25 February she writes just three words: 'Francis left Mollie.' Mollie was Marion Cooke, Russell's second wife.

Russell returned to the chalet in March and Elizabeth recorded, 'Francis & I very happy ... Lovely day. Walked with Francis to new hotel – lay in sun. P.M. lay in sun in our old place near chalet.'

Although Elizabeth longed for intimacy, she knew she had 'no real gift for the married state', the difficulties of which are the preoccupation of most of her novels. In the spring of 1914, she wrote to Francis to say, 'once a widow always a widow' and then added that she thought it best, 'after a certain age, to leave well alone'. Francis responded by asking her to define the word 'well'.

Easter brought 'heavenly soft warm weather – everything too beautiful'. But the glorious sunshine was marred by discord with her teenage daughter Felicitas, whom she nicknamed Martin. 'Perfectly heavenly hot blue scented day, Martin spoiling it by being rude and horrid to Teppi and devilish in fact.' The next day Martin is again 'being a surprising nuisance'.

For the following week Elizabeth suffers from 'violent tummyaches', which may have been caused by anxiety. After Felicitas left to return to school in late April, Elizabeth appears to recover. But then in June, her difficult daughter interrupts Elizabeth's newfound happiness again. The following entries in the diary are cryptic:

> *10 June*: Mlle Bollinger wrote I was to go at once and remove Martin who has stolen money again. Francis took me to Lausanne. Interviews at Chateau des Apennins.
> *11 June*: Rushed round Lausanne and environs with Francis to doctors etc to find a place for Martin. Came home to tea.
> *12 June*: Sent Teppi to Corneaux Sanatorium above Montreux where Bollingers had put Martin.
> *16 June*: Greatly perturbed about finding a place for Martin – many telegrams.

The ostensible story is that Felicitas, while at boarding school, had stolen money and been expelled, which resulted in her mother having to find another boarding school nearby that would take her. In the interim, Felicitas was installed in a local hospital and rehabilitation centre (which still exists as the Clinique Valmont, now a health retreat for the super wealthy). The ever-faithful Teppi was sent to Corneaux sur Montreux to fetch the allegedly misbehaving daughter and Elizabeth records that: 'They came back to supper' and endured a 'horrid and degrading evening with Martin'.

The horrid and degrading scenes ended in Elizabeth sending her daughter away again without a farewell and, as extra punishment, forbidding her to play the piano. Felicitas was a gifted musician, like her mother, and playing the piano was possibly one of the few joys left to her as she drifted from one institution to the next. Given all the children had spent many years vying for attention from their mother, Felicitas's expulsion from the chalet must have been doubly painful when it coincided with the arrival of Elizabeth's favoured daughter, Liebet.

Teppi assumed the job of taking Felicitas to Marburg, presumably leaving the child feeling that she had not only been expelled from her school, but also from her family. The Usborne biography alleges that Felicitas later wrote her mother a letter saying she 'hoped never to see her again'. All we know for certain is that their very last meeting was traumatic and tempestuous.

Soon after, Elizabeth was swept up with the outbreak of war and the diary of that year does not mention Martin again.

The news of the assassination of Archduke Franz Ferdinand came casually in late June. Elizabeth was enjoying a summer walk from Alpino to Orta in 'hot and heavenly' weather when she 'met Italian on way who told us of blown up Austrian Archduke'. The next day she seems unperturbed as she goes boating at Orta all day. 'Leib bathed. I lay and read poets. Lovely moon.'

But the rumours of war and Germany mobilising soon disturbed the beautiful alpine summer. By August, the Deutsche

Bank, where Elizabeth kept her money, had shut. Swiss troops seized supplies from the local trains and soon the chalet was left with little more than potatoes and cheese, while the locals were already suffering from hunger. The house of happiness had transformed into a house of want and fear. Francis wrote to Elizabeth advising her to leave for England as soon as possible. On 6 August, she records in her diary: 'Burnt papers, arranged things for flight if necessary.'

Arrangements necessitated obtaining false passports. She fled with her two daughters Liebet and Evi carrying nothing more than a handbag and a knapsack. From Geneva, they travelled to Paris and then 'left for Havre by a miracle. Got safe on steamer at night – all night on deck.' On this final leg of the journey, the girls were instructed not to talk in case somebody heard their German accents.

Arriving in England in September Elizabeth was 'fearfully happy' and went directly to the foreign office to arrange her naturalisation. Without it, she could be considered an alien. She quickly reunited with Francis and they spent Christmas together at Telegraph House, his estate in County Sussex, the first Christmas Elizabeth had ever spent away from her children. According to her diary, she and Francis are 'both very happy'.

'So ends 1914,' she writes finally, 'it has been the happiest year of my life.'

As Elizabeth spent more time with Francis her lover's extreme moods became obvious, often swinging from boyish gaiety to tyrannical bullying in a single morning. Elizabeth's moods swung in tandem; one moment in love, the next in despair. Nevertheless, she spent much of 1915 struggling to maintain the love affair, while simultaneously suffering serious doubts about the relationship and reiterating to Francis the 'hopelessness of marriage'. These doubts she also confessed to Francis's brother, Bertrand, which he in turn reported to Lady Ottoline Morrell, his own mistress of the time:

> She says – and I believe her – that she was unguarded with my brother at first, because she looked upon him as safely married and therefore suitable as a lover. Suddenly, without consulting her, he wrote and said he was getting divorced … Now she is feeling very worried because the inexorable moment is coming when his divorce will be absolute and she will have to decide. Her objections to him are the following: a) he sleeps with seven dogs on his bed … b) he reads Kipling aloud; c) he loves Telegraph House which is hideous … She would be delighted to go on having him for a lover, but I feel sure he will never agree to that.

Despite her very real misgivings, Elizabeth believed she was in love, and on 11 February 1916, following the finalisation of Russell's divorce, the couple married. It was a Friday and for the rest of her life Fridays would always be associated with foreboding. By Easter the press had picked up the story. The news of one of England's most popular novelists marrying the grandson of a former UK Prime Minister who had already been married twice, and tried once for bigamy, was a story worth chasing. The newlyweds found themselves pursued and fled to Cornwall for privacy.

In the days following her wedding Elizabeth discovered, for the second time, that marriage vows can have the effect of dramatically changing a relationship for the worse. She confessed later to her friend George Santayana that Francis was 'very different as a lover from what he was as a husband'.

On the couple's return to Telegraph House, Elizabeth was feeling so bereft that she escaped to a little tin shed in the grounds which she called her 'hutch', and noted in her journal 'the complete incompatibility of us two wretched mortals'. Her husband was so controlling that he forbade her to leave the property without his permission. When the couple then travelled to London Elizabeth was further appalled when Francis spent the evening at his club playing bridge, leaving her alone in a hotel. She had no idea, at that stage, that her new husband was a serious gambler, even though long before their wedding he had borrowed money from her, which he admitted losing at bridge. Neither did she realise he was a cocaine-user and a philanderer.

At this point, Elizabeth may well have been deciding to abandon the marriage but just when she might have gathered the strength to leave, tragedy intervened. News arrived that her favourite nephew had been killed in the war, and she immediately rushed off to comfort her sister, Charlotte. At her sister's house another telegram arrived containing even worse news: Elizabeth's estranged sixteen-year-old daughter Felicitas – pretty, talented and possibly the daughter who most resembled her mother – had died. The grieving mother returned to her husband to fall once again into the strong masculine arms she mistakenly believed would console and protect her.

The facts around Felicitas's death, like the facts around her life, are blurry. The initial telegram did not state the cause. Only later was the reason provided: double pneumonia. The young girl had been taken out of her boarding school, according to Usborne, because her funds had been frozen in the banks and she was unable to pay the fees. Teppi came to the rescue and arranged for Felicitas to work in a children's hospital in Bremen, but somewhere in the transition Elizabeth's youngest daughter had fallen fatally ill.

In a letter to Liebet announcing the news of the double tragedy Elizabeth wrote:

> I've got sad news for you – Johnnie was killed in the naval battle and the same day we heard that, came a telegram from Teppi saying briefly and giving no explanation that Martin is dead. My precious little Liebet, how dreadful to have to tell you this … My little Martin! The pitifulness of it all alone there without her Mummy and only sixteen …

She ends the letter with a postscript:

> I think it best that you and Evi should tell no one of
> this, and not therefore, be forced to go into mourning
> and all that nonsense. You can explain when you want
> to be quiet that a very dear cousin was killed – which
> is also only too true.

Usborne describes the cause of Felicitas's illness thus: 'the child
had been playing the violin in front of an open window wearing
damp clothing and had collapsed with double pneumonia'.

On hearing of the collapse and subsequent hospitalisation,
Teppi, as her surrogate mother, rushed to Felicitas's bedside.
She was assured by the doctors that the young girl would
survive and subsequently left her for the night. Early the next
morning, utterly alone, Felicitas breathed her last.

Elizabeth wrote to Teppi:

> No one knows better than you how shattered I must
> be ... because of everything that preceded this, because
> of my thoughts of the last time I saw Martin, leaving
> for ever and ever, without a kiss, without love, after the
> sad scenes of the last days of the chalet. If only I had
> held her in my arms once again! To tell her how deeply
> I loved her, and that it was just because I loved her so
> that I suffered so greatly on account of what she had
> done. Teppi, how can anyone bear such things?

I am not entirely convinced by the story of Felicitas's manner of death. The image of the young violinist by the open window fatally collapsing sounds far too romantic and operatic to be true, unless her immune system was already severely compromised. And pneumonia is contracted through a virus, not through damp clothes or cool draughts. It seems mysterious that someone so young could contract pneumonia in mid-summer and die so quickly, and it is curious that Elizabeth instructed her daughters Liebet and Evi not to tell anybody the news. Also barely credible is the idea that Elizabeth 'suffered so greatly' on account of her daughter's misdemeanour – allegedly stealing half a crown – a crime that Felicitas went to her deathbed disavowing. If that story is to be believed, Elizabeth fought with her daughter and banished her to a remote boarding school all for the sake of two and a half shillings. The motherly outrage, surely, had to be over something more substantial.

As a child in Lausanne, Elizabeth had experienced a scandal in the Beauchamp family that may possibly have been echoed in the scandal of Felicitas. When Elizabeth was eight years old, her extremely pretty fifteen-year-old sister, Charlotte, fell pregnant. The young girl was removed from society, gave birth to a child who was also removed, and then returned home, presumably on the condition that the incident was never mentioned again. Is it possible that Felicitas was urgently removed from her boarding school for the same reason? Is that why Madame Bollinger sent her to a sanatorium and also why Elizabeth recorded in her diary having to consult with 'doctors etc'? Could this explain Felicitas's debilitated physical condition?

The reason given for Elizabeth's daughter's removal from the second boarding school – due to Felicitas's funds being frozen – is also unconvincing. If Felicitas had funds of her own, why did she need to steal half a crown? Afterwards, when Teppi was going through the young girl's belongings, she found a diary 'which reiterated that she had not stolen the half-crown she had been punished for'. None of it seems to add up.

It is possible that the visit to see Swiss doctors may have involved a psychiatric consultation. Elizabeth's sister, Charlotte, had a son who had been committed to what Elizabeth described as 'a lunatic asylum' and ultimately suicided. Mental illness may have been in the family. Again, it is unlikely that the true story will ever be known. Almost all the letters and diary entries in relation to this episode have been expunged from the surviving papers. Clearly, this was a tragedy about which Elizabeth preferred to leave as little documentation as possible.

It is impossible to gauge the regret Elizabeth must have felt or the guilt that would inevitably engulf a mother whose child had died alone and estranged. The only explanation available is the novel she wrote as a result of the tragedy, *Christine*, and that, in the end, turns out to be a curious and consummate cover-up.

Christine was published in 1917 under the pseudonym Alice Cholmondeley. Elizabeth always denied she was the author, even to her closest friends. The book is entirely composed of letters from a daughter to her mother just prior to the outbreak of war, correspondence which the preface claims to be genuine, and some of which were direct transcriptions of letters between Felicitas and Elizabeth.

> My daughter Christine who wrote me these letters, died at a hospital in Stuttgart on the morning of August 8th, 1914, of acute double pneumonia. I have kept these letters private for almost three years, because, apart from the love in them that made them sacred things ... they seemed to me ... too extreme and sweeping in their judgments. Now, as the years have passed ... I feel that these letters ... may have a certain value in helping to put together a small corner of the great picture of Germany which it will be necessary to keep clear and naked before us in the future if the world is to be saved ... The war killed Christine, just as surely as if she had been a soldier in the trenches.

This last statement is almost identical to the one that Elizabeth wrote in a letter to her elder daughter in the immediate aftermath of Felicitas's death. She clearly convinced herself that the war was entirely to blame for her youngest daughter's premature passing.

The final paragraph of the preface to Christine states: 'I never saw her again. I had a telegram saying she was dead.

I tried to go to Stuttgart, but was turned back at the frontier.' The first two sentences are true in relation to the circumstances around Felicitas's death; the last is not. In hindsight, Elizabeth probably wished that she had at least attempted to go to her daughter's side in the aftermath of the devastating news but that did not happen. In fact, the entire book is a re-writing of the mother-and-daughter history, an invention of a relationship full of intimacy and devotion that the author imagined might have been – rather than what it really was. Writing *Christine* was the writer's way of recovering from her deep grief and of explaining – and maybe excusing – her own role in the death of her daughter.

The epistolary novel begins with:

My blessed little Mother,
Here I am safe, and before I unpack or do a thing I'm writing you a little line of love.

The set-up is that Christine, a promising violinist, has travelled to Germany at great cost and sacrifice, to study with a German master of the instrument in the hope that she will one day develop a career as a musician. She lives in a boarding house while attending violin lessons with the famous maestro Kloster, and every Sunday she writes to her beloved mother, bearing witness to the intensely war-hungry mood of her household, her town and the country at large. What interests me most is not Christine's account of political events however – an apparently realistic record that beguiled reviewers – but her personal comments and the emotional portrait drawn of the mother–daughter relationship.

Immediately, the mirroring of Elizabeth's own life is obvious. Among her extensive array of talents was musicianship and perfect pitch, and the author may well have become a professional organist if she had been born at a time when females were allowed to pursue their musical talents beyond the drawing room. Felicitas had inherited her mother's ability, not only at the keyboard but also with stringed instruments.

The first letter from Christine continues:

> ... the moment I've had a bath and tidied up I shall get out my fiddle and see if I've forgotten how to play it between London and Berlin. If only I can be sure you aren't going to be too lonely! Beloved mother, it will only be a year, or even less if I work fearfully hard ... Oh, I know you'll write and tell me you don't mind a bit ... but you see your Chris hasn't lived with you all her life for nothing; she knows you very well now, at least, as much of your dear sacred self that you will show her.

This tone of daughterly adoration continues throughout the entire book. It is difficult not to conclude that Elizabeth is using her virtuosic imagination to re-live, re-cast and re-write the greatest tragedy in her life, the only way perhaps of surviving her deep bereavement. The reality was just too terrible; she had to invent a fiction to replace it.

I know you're going to be brave and all that but one can be very unhappy while one is being brave, and besides, one isn't brave unless one is suffering.

This sentence reflects the sentiments of the letter that Elizabeth sent to her daughter Liebet following the news of Felicitas's death:

> … my poor Martin – it's too dreadful – I can't bear it – and yet I am going to bear it, and you dear other crabs are going to help by being absolutely quietly courageous over it … Liebet darling, don't fret – if you crabs will only hold out and set your teeth and look forward to the happy times that certainly will come, then so can I. But if you aren't able to then I feel that neither shall I be able to. So remember that, won't you, my little blessed crab.

In the novel, the young Christine displays some obvious Elizabeth-like tastes and personality traits, which may well have been characteristics of the young Felicitas also. As a young pianist, Elizabeth had excelled at playing Bach. Indeed, it was on hearing her play the fugues that Henning had fallen in love with her. And she also had a lifelong fondness for the poetry of Wordsworth. In *Christine*, the daughter writes to her mother: 'I don't know why I always think of Bach first when I write about music as I think of Wordsworth first when I think of poetry …'

And then she adds, with Elizabeth-style optimism and rapture:

> What a world it is, my sweetest little mother! It is so full of beauty ... I do think it's a splendid world, full of glory created in the past and lighting us up while we create still greater glory. One has only got to shut out the parts of the present one doesn't like to see this all clear and feel so happy.

Elizabeth, during 1916, was also trying to shut out the parts of the present she didn't like. Most of all she was trying to shut out the reality of her broken relationship with her daughter, by inventing a kind of pseudo-Felicitas, whose musical promise, instead of being cruelly cut off, had been encouraged.

Another letter from Christine says:

> It is so wonderful, your happiness in my being happy, so touching. I'm all melted with love and gratitude when I think of it, and of the dear way you let me do this, come away here and realise my dream of studying ... I just want to say good-night, and tell you, in case you shouldn't have noticed it, how much your daughter loves you.

There are many little asides throughout this smokescreen of a novel that hint at the real-life events that brought *Christine* into being. One lonely Sunday, the young violinist is caught playing on the day of the week when all gaieties such as music are prohibited in Germany and she admits in a letter to her mother that 'I was very much ashamed of myself, besides feeling as though I were fifteen and caught at school doing something wicked.'

The mother, who remains unnamed, is an idealised version of Elizabeth, the mother she wished she had been, and the love between mother and daughter is so intense as to be unbelievable, the adoration occasionally rising to the tone of religious worship.

> Why are you so dear, my darling mother? If you were an ordinary mother I'd be so much more placid … It's only that I love you. We're such *friends*. You always understand, you are never shocked. I can say whatever comes into my head to you. It is as good as saying one's prayers.

It is at this point that the reader would be forgiven for doubting Elizabeth's own mental stability; such a mother–daughter relationship, even if it *were* real, would be profoundly unhealthy. My interpretation is that deep grief can be a form of madness and this was Elizabeth's particular manifestation of her overwhelming bereavement.

Later Christine comments: 'I'm sure that's why we've been so happy together, because you've never taken anything I've done or said that was foolish or unkind *personally*.'

Clearly, whatever crime Felicitas had committed, Elizabeth *had* taken it personally, and their relationship had not been characterised by happiness. And yet, if even only a few of these letters from Christine were actual transcriptions of Felicitas's letters to her mother, there is enough evidence to show that, despite conflict, there was a genuine and deep love between them. In essence, *Christine* is an attempt to make amends with the dead, and is a long letter of regret. But isn't parenting, by its very nature, a territory of regret? The fact that Elizabeth could eventually forgive herself and return to periods of happiness demonstrates a rare resilience and a powerful quality of spirit.

I too have spent a good deal of my life writing love letters to the dead. The first was a letter to my father after his suicide, which was essentially a eulogy that ended with a message of forgiveness and turned into the book *In My Father's House*. By the time I'd finished, I had almost recovered from my grief. Twenty years later, I wrote a letter to my beloved mother, *Waiting Room*, whose death led me directly to my next book, also inspired by letters, between my mother and the Australian novelist and poet, Randolph Stow, an author I wrote to before *and* after he died. And my obsession with letters didn't stop there. When I discovered an archive of hundreds of letters written by adoring young readers to Ivan Southall, I wrote a tribute to the man who was my favourite childhood author and my very first literary kindred spirit. Most recently, I wrote an essay-length letter addressed to James Joyce, the author who has influenced me most of all, which starts: 'Dear Jim ...' and informs the great Irishman that I am resigning my position as chief *Finnegans Wake* fangirl because his demand that a reader 'should devote his whole Life to reading my works' was just a bit like being married to a very demanding husband.

In fact, I've spent so much time writing to and reading about dead people that sometimes I feel like Mrs Fisher in *The Enchanted April*, who prefers the company of the noble departed to the living. And yet here I am again, writing an impassioned fan letter to a woman I will never meet. I know that Elizabeth enjoyed having adorers so I like to think that she would appreciate an Australian author, albeit untitled and commercially unsuccessful, attempting to resurrect her literary legacy.

There was much speculation about the origin of *Christine* but Elizabeth's publishers refused to identify the writer, insisting that the manuscript had arrived in their offices anonymously and that all communication with the author had gone through a lawyer.

Reviewers and readers were undecided about whether Christine was completely factual or partly fictional. The book was generally received as a genuine first-person testimony of the increasingly bellicose mood that engulfed the German nation in the lead-up to World War I but some critics were confused by the author's genre-bending. *Punch* magazine was 'perplexed – and a little provoked' by the way in which the narrative was presented – advertised as a novel and yet claiming the veracity of the letters. The reviewer concluded, as did many others, that Miss Cholmondeley 'was herself in Germany during the summer of 1914, and has chosen this way of telling us what she saw and heard'. In the United States *The Nation* stated that, 'If it is a genuine record it is too important to pass, as it may in many minds, as fiction.' *The New York Times* collected information from other newspapers and listed the *New York Tribune* and *New York Post* as being among those who believed *Christine* was 'an important historical document'.

The British periodical *Land and Water* considered the book was a factual account, even suggesting that it was 'one of the most vital and intense condemnations of Germany that has been or will be produced'. The *Times Literary Supplement* commented that is was difficult to believe that the book was 'written by any but an eye witness' and *The Daily Telegraph* maintained that the book was so realistic as to leave no doubt that its author wrote from actual experience. Finally, *The Nation* stated that if the letters proved genuine then the book would become 'a document as significant as any the war has yet furnished'.

The attention the book received was all focused on its value as a wartime documentary; nobody saw it as a deep psychological study. The curious fact about *Christine* is that the novel may have more insight into the author than any other and yet it is probably the least read of von Arnim's works.

On returning to Telegraph House in June 1916 to deliver her terrible news about her daughter, Elizabeth records that 'F. was very kind and dear' and 'that night we reached a communion we haven't had since we married so that I felt happy in spite of sorrow'.

Three days later she records being 'so glad and thankful to be with him again' after Francis arrived home late from a bridge game. But then in characteristic tyrannical style, her husband fell into a rage with a servant because she had failed to put a towel in his room and Elizabeth 'collapsed into wretched tears of despair'. The following day the diary notes:

> Telegraph House & misery – the misery of Martin's death and Tit's loss and here F. being determined in his incomprehensions – no sense whatever of values – angry with me for being miserable over his row last night. I got down to the very dregs today of hopeless misery.

Less than a week after hearing the news of her daughter's death, Francis was behaving in a way that Elizabeth describes as 'unkind and inhuman'. When she needed him most, her husband was unable to tear himself away from his nightly bridge game at his club.

'If F. would only understand and keep a little close to me these days but he can't for a day not go away to his bridge playing leaving me to eat out my heart alone.'

This was a sign of cold-heartedness in the extreme but also a clear indication of addiction. Among other things, Francis

Russell was addicted to gambling and servicing his addictions took precedence over all else.

Fortunately, the arrival of George Santayana at Telegraph House obliged Francis to behave in a more civil manner and briefly lifted Elizabeth's spirits. As a regular visitor during 1916, Santayana later wrote his recollections of Elizabeth:

> She found it necessary to set up a bungalow of her own, where no one was allowed to disturb her ... This was the first symptom of domestic division that came to my notice; but ultimately she began frankly to confess the difficulties she found in living with Russell.

By the end of 1916 Elizabeth concluded her diary by stating, 'This year was the most wretched of my life. I have never been so unhappy as from February to September.' Yet again, her life had bounced between extremes; 1914 had been her happiest and only two years later, she has sunk into misery. Elizabeth ended the wretchedness temporarily by secretly fleeing to America, where her daughter Liebet had settled. It would take another three years before she summoned the strength to leave Francis for good after realising he was having an affair with his secretary, Miss Otter, as well as discovering 'behaviour of a secret nature that made it impossible for a decent woman to stay'. This behaviour may have been the discovery of her husband's bisexuality, combined with his drug addictions. Typically discreet, Elizabeth provides no details.

Many years later Elizabeth confessed to a lifelong friend that perhaps she hadn't really been in love with Francis but she had *believed* she was and hadn't understood the difference between believing and the genuine feeling. I can well understand such doubts and have similarly duped myself on many occasions. Being in love is such a blessed place to be that it is tempting to convince oneself that you're in it even when you are not. Illusion and self-delusion are two areas in which writers excel, as if the boundary between imagination and reality is in a constant state of negotiation between two blind cartographers.

Elizabeth was forty-eight when she allowed 'Doom' to step into her Swiss home and fed him legs of mutton even though she preferred poached eggs. At the time she had been widowed for three years, had experienced loneliness, and perhaps believed this was her final chance for lasting companionship.

Oddly, I was the same age when I fell for the very last in my long line of unsuitable suitors – a seductively handsome man, twelve years younger, who proclaimed deep and lasting love, and then proceeded to transform into a violent, possessive tyrant. When we met I also felt a deep gravitational pull that seemed so strong I believed it was predestined. And perhaps like Elizabeth after the loss of her daughter, I was also in the throes of grief, after witnessing my mother's painful death from stomach cancer. I too had no strength to resist what was being offered: a devoted 'rock-like' support and continued avowals of 'love', which was actually a masquerade for something else completely. As if this wasn't contradiction enough, I was also surprised to discover a strange but distinct connection between deep grief and powerful sex. Or perhaps I mean the strangely healing power of sex – of bodies rather than words – on that inexpressible state we call bereavement. And perhaps this is why Elizabeth had noted, on the night of hearing about the death of Felicitas, that there had been happiness within the misery – she had been consoled by deep sex.

Lord Russell's final attempt at revenge was to sue the removalist firm that Elizabeth had engaged to pick up her belongings from Telegraph House. Francis accused the removalists, and by implication his wife, of taking items that were his, including cushions, electric light fittings, tennis balls and a hammock. This led to a legal process that was protracted and expensive for both parties, and also provided rich material for the gossip press, including the reporting of a lengthy cross-examination over who had bought a hammock and with what purpose.

> Q: Now about the hammock. You bought the hammock
> on the 17th April 1916?
> A: Yes.
> Q: Is it a suitable hammock for Lord Russell?
> A: No.
> Q: Did you ever give it to him?
> A: Never.

Q: You have more regard for life?
A: And for the hammock.

Once the legal proceedings in relation to her separation were over, Lady Russell, as she was now known, 'crawled' back to her chalet to recover. There Elizabeth began working on her next anonymously published book, *In the Mountains*, which stands out from her other novels as far more experimental and modernist in style. The story is told in first person by a woman who escapes to the mountains to recover from a disturbing event, the details of which are never given, although we gather it has something to do with a failed romance. 'Presently you'll reach the stage when you begin to realise that falling out of love is every bit as agreeable as falling in,' a friend advises the forlorn protagonist. 'It is, you know. It's a wonderful feeling, that gradual restoration to freedom and one's friends.'

Although the author did, in typical stout-hearted style, soon recover her sunny temperament, the haranguing from her estranged husband continued for at least another two years. Francis's parting shot was to send his once-beloved a copy of the Bible with every reference to faithless wives underlined. Bertrand Russell, however, supported his sister-in-law throughout the separation, writing to her from Dorset in July 1919:

> It is quite hateful to think your being so tormented and battered. I wish you were coming here to listen to the sea on the rocks and watch the gulls sailing through

the sky. But the chalet ought to be healing. Now I hope you have done with F. Remember how many gay and delicious things there are in the world – don't forget that you have won liberty, which is worth a price – and that you can build up friendships with people who will appreciate you without wanting to destroy you.
Yours affectionately, BR.

'F. continues to lie & say I lie –' Elizabeth wrote back to her brother-in-law the following year, '& dictates the most intimate insults to me to his secretary, & sends copies of them round to people.'

Bertrand writes again from Peking in 1921, saying that his brother had shown him the letters he had sent to Elizabeth and he thought them 'unspeakably horrible'; he'd also had 'a savage letter from Frank saying I was writing to you and seeing you and behaving, as always, disloyally to him'. He ends the letter, 'but I don't think, my dear sister-in-law, you need worry on the score of Devil' (their nickname for Frank). 'Goodbye with much love, yours affectionately, Bertrand Russell.'

Elizabeth nevertheless seems to have been haunted by her second husband for years to come. More than a decade later, and long after Francis died, she was still attempting to understand the 'Devil's' personality by searching for answers in his childhood, which had been marred by tragedy, his mother and sister dying of diphtheria, followed by his father, John Russell, two years later. In 1937 Bertrand responded to her enquiry about his brother's character while they were growing up. 'Yes, Frank as a boy seems just like what he was later; one gets an impression that it was nature, not bad education.' The letter was signed 'Bertie'.

🌿

While living in London in the spring of 1920, Elizabeth wrote to her younger cousin Katherine Mansfield and arranged to visit her in Hampstead for tea. This was not a meeting of equals. Elizabeth was full of robust health, fabulously wealthy and the author of twelve best-selling novels; Katherine was impoverished, constantly ill and had only just published her second collection of stories.

Elizabeth was keen to reacquaint herself with her cousin because Mansfield had published a positive review of von Arnim's most recent novel, *Christopher and Columbus*. 'She is, in the happiest way, conscious of her own particular vision, and wants no other,' Mansfield concluded. 'In a world where there are so many furies with warning fingers it is good to know of someone who goes her own way finding a gay garland.'

Despite her apparent regard for von Arnim as a writer, Mansfield wasn't looking forward to their tête é tête, complaining in a letter to a friend that 'a thousand devils are sending Elizabeth without her German Garden to tea here tomorrow ... she will be, Oh, such a little bundle of artificialities – but I can't put her off.'

Mansfield's impression of artificiality was not unfounded. Elizabeth worked hard at creating her persona, perhaps even a variety of personas. In her book *The Merry Wives of Westminster*, Belloc Lowndes, who considered Elizabeth 'a genius', also believed she had two distinct sides. 'As I grew to know her really well, I realised she had a dual – what is now called a split – personality.' Clearly, Elizabeth had distinct aspects of her personality. She could be silent and withdrawn, as noted by Walpole, and also seductively charming while regularly shocking people with her frankness. Over tea, Elizabeth was perhaps too frank with her young cousin because Katherine later complained in her journal that she thought her older cousin had 'a vulgar little mind'.

In contrast, Elizabeth went away from their meeting deeply impressed and 'inspired to write something that was not filled with gay garlands'. Her conversation with her younger cousin had deepened her literary ambitions and she went directly to her Swiss chalet where, twelve days later, she began drafting the creation of her most profound work.

Vera was the first book of Elizabeth's I read. It is also her darkest. And, in my view, her masterpiece. A haunting portrait of psychological tyranny, her thirteenth novel precisely and terrifyingly portrays the nature of domestic violence without ever having the perpetrator raise his fist. At the time of my first reading, I had just separated from an extremely controlling partner so this book spoke to me like a dear and deeply comforting friend. Elizabeth seemed to understand exactly what I had been through. More than that, as she was capable of finding the comedy in any situation, despite the tragedy and brutality, *Vera* still made me laugh.

The heroine of *Vera* is twenty-two-year-old Lucy who, on the day of her father's death, meets the much older Everard Wemyss (pronounced Weems). When Wemyss invites himself into her garden, invading her physical space as well as her private mourning, Lucy is still in a state of shock. In contemporary terms, we might say she has temporarily lost all boundaries. It is while in this state of extreme vulnerability that Wemyss falls violently and possessively in love with her, and Lucy feels, as Elizabeth did with Francis, that at a time of great sadness and uncertainty she has found a 'tower of strength and rock of refuge'. Perhaps being suddenly fatherless, Lucy also felt unanchored, as many women do without a man attached to them. (Betty, wife of Don Draper, the serial philanderer in *Mad Men*, confides to her friend while pondering separation from her husband: 'Without him, I feel I will just float away'. And Julia, in Edward St Aubyn's *Mother's Milk* comments: 'Since divorcing Richard I get these horrible moments of vertigo. I suddenly feel as if I don't exist.')

Wemyss is also in a state of grief, but of a very different kind. His wife, Vera, has recently died in an accident – falling to her death from the second-storey window of their country home, her body smashing onto the terrace directly in front of her husband. A coronial enquiry, widely reported in the newspapers, has left an open verdict, suggesting a possible suicide. To avoid the gossip in London Wemyss has escaped to Cornwall, where Lucy has recently arrived with her father for the summer. He is not grieving his wife so much as his reputation. Indeed, he is clearly irritated by what he believes was his wife's deliberate carelessness. 'Imagine bringing such horror to him, such unforgettable horror, besides worries and unhappiness without end, by deliberately disregarding his warnings, his orders indeed, about that window.'

At their very first meeting Lucy feels that Wemyss has 'the quality of an irresistible natural phenomenon', 'like some elemental force', just as Elizabeth had felt with Francis. Their shared condition of bereavement indicates to Lucy that 'Death himself had been their introducer,' and death, like doom, the author suggests, is a predestination no woman can deny.

In the aftermath of the funeral Wemyss pursues Lucy and they are married quietly to avoid a society that disapproves of a widower re-marrying within the established one-year mourning period. (Lucy's aunt is particularly offended by Wemyss wearing grey, rather than black trousers.)

After their wedding, Lucy finds that marriage is 'different from what she had supposed'. One can only assume that the disillusionment suffered by Lucy during her honeymoon also reflected Elizabeth's:

> ... she hadn't been married a week before she was reflecting what a bad arrangement it was, the way ecstasy seemed to have no staying power. Also it oughtn't to begin, she considered, at its topmost height and accordingly not be able to move except downwards. If one could only start modestly in marriage with very little of it and work steadily upwards ...

Because Lucy's nights are now continually interrupted – although the author refrains from saying by what exactly – the newlywed young woman also has the added discomfort of always being tired. The other big difference in her life is that 'she was never alone'. Previously: 'Always there had been places she could go to and rest in quietly, safe from interruption; now there were none ... you were never, day or night, an instant off duty.'

In Elizabeth's correspondence with her publishers – (she was on a first-name basis with Sir Frederick Macmillan) – there was some disagreement about the title. The author insisted on *Vera*, which is easily assimilated into Wemyss's given name, Everard, and cleverly foreshadows Lucy's fate. The novel progresses subtly and slowly as we witness Lucy steadily reduced until she is wholly consumed by her avaricious and controlling husband, a triumph gained under the guise of love.

'We shan't know where one ends and the other begins,' Everard announces to Lucy delightedly. 'That, little Love, is a real marriage.' Although Lucy readily concurs with her husband that 'real marriage' means 'agreeing whole-heartedly to have no concealments', she soon realises that in reality 'a doubt in her mind was better kept there'.

After their honeymoon, the couple take up residence in The Willows, Wemyss's country home, which strongly resembles Francis Russell's Telegraph House. At The Willows, Wemyss suggests that he and his new young wife can take tea on the terrace, exactly where Vera had been found 'smashed'.

Lucy has learnt by then not to speak her mind, her thoughts remain unvoiced: 'The tea would taste of blood.'

In a letter to her daughter Liebet, Elizabeth von Arnim wrote saying she knew that *Vera* was her 'high watermark' and that she would 'never write anything as good again', but she had no wish to do so for 'it was extracted from me by torment'. (She did, however, enjoy overhearing a woman at one of Hugh Walpole's parties hissing to her husband: 'Don't you go Weemsing me.')

When *Vera* was published in September 1921 it was received with confusion by many readers and reviewers. The playful, witty Elizabeth von Arnim, author of light social comedies and often likened to Jane Austen, had been mysteriously transfigured into a gothic writer of macabre tragedy. When the first uncomplimentary review appeared in the *Times Literary Supplement*, John Middleton Murry is reported to have commented: 'Of course my dear, when the critics are faced with *Wuthering Heights* by Jane Austen, they don't know what to say.' Elizabeth had deliberately referenced Brontë's book in several ways: when Lucy first arrives at The Willows the branches outside the window make 'a loud irregular tapping'; and Lucy reads Vera's copy of *Wuthering Heights* even though her husband disapproves of it as morbid.

Other reviews were more favourable. The *Daily Express*

called *Vera* 'this famous writer's masterpiece' while Rebecca West called it 'a triumph', describing Elizabeth as 'a sort of sparkling Euclid which nobody can touch' and *Vera* 'the most successful attempt at the macabre in English', insisting that 'there is no real reason why a book should not be just as tragic as comic'. *The New York Times* described the tale as the 'story of a modern Bluebeard' and in the *London Mercury* Edward Shanks believed Wemyss was 'probably the most monstrous egoist in all literature'. The *Literary Review* stated:

> Only a woman, only a married woman, only a married English woman, could have written it. It is a work of the highest art, and one instinctively recalls Jane Austen's masterly portraits.

And of Wemyss, the reviewer notes: 'All men have something of him in them ...'

Francis Russell's response to the publication of *Vera* was outrage. In his literary reminiscences, Frank Swinnerton writes that, '*Vera* was the talk of the town' and that 'Russell must have recognised scenes which had really occurred'. George Santayana, having been a regular visitor at Telegraph House, recorded that 'many of the details are photographic: and it was, perhaps, cruel to publish them during his life-time. But he had driven her to desperation; and she developed the spite of a hunted animal.'

The estranged ex-husband carried a copy of the book with him around London 'accosting people at his club and demanding to know if they thought it contained true descriptions of himself'. Then he threatened a libel action and Macmillan received writs from his solicitors. Russell was eventually persuaded by his lawyers to drop the case but he then switched to suing his wife for desertion and employed private detectives to uncover evidence of adultery. All the rumours, once out to the general public, only led to increasing book sales.

ยุ่

On reading *Vera*, Katherine Mansfield wrote to a friend: 'Isn't the end extraordinarily good? ... Have you never known a Wemyss? Oh, my dear, they are *very* plentiful! Few men are without a touch.' When the friend suggested that Elizabeth may have been influenced by Mansfield, the younger writer's response was as follows: 'My hand on heart, I could swear to: never *could* Elizabeth be influenced by me.' And yet in reality, it turns out that we may have Katherine Mansfield to thank for inspiring Elizabeth to rise to her own occasion, producing the finest work of her entire career.

The influence did not flow in one direction only. In Kathleen Jones's 2010 biography of Mansfield she describes Elizabeth as the younger writer's 'role model' and admits that she 'may have had a considerable influence on Katherine's early work'. It was upon reading *Elizabeth and her German Garden* at the age of ten that Katherine decided to become a writer. Later, as a celebrity author, the more established writer did much to raise awareness of her cousin's work among literary circles. While attending Queen's College in London, Mansfield was inspired by *The Adventures of Elizabeth in Rugen* to write what would be her first published story, 'Die Einsame', translated as 'The Lonely One', which was also a site on the island of Rugen visited by Elizabeth. The story opens with a description of a woman who sounds a little like Elizabeth herself:

> All alone she was. All alone with her soul. She lived on the top of a solitary hill. Her house was small and bare, and alone, too. All day long she spent in the forest, with the trees and the flowers and the birds. She seemed like a creature of the forest herself, sometimes.

Towards the end of her life, Mansfield wrote to Elizabeth: 'I would like to write one story really good enough to offer you one day.' On writing 'The Garden Party', Katherine lived up to her older cousin's high expectations and Elizabeth wrote to a friend: 'I'm fearfully proud of her – just as if I had hatched her.'

Scholar Isobel Maddison believes that, 'Given the evidence, it seems deliberately perverse not to believe that she did.' Mansfield's first collection of stories, *In a German Pension*, for example, is preoccupied with themes similar to Elizabeth's first 'German' novels and both have been categorised as anti-invasion literature.

The two cousins felt a deep kinship but there was friction as well. When Elizabeth responded to Katherine's 'At the Bay' by describing it as 'a pretty little story', for example, Mansfield retaliated with her story 'A Cup of Tea' – about a middle-aged wealthy aristocrat taking pity on a poor, uneducated younger woman – evidence of what Maddison describes as 'a literary flashpoint' in their relationship. Elizabeth later apologised for her comment, in her typically generous-hearted fashion.

The big difference between the cousins was the level of recognition afforded to Elizabeth von Arnim, who was celebrated during her lifetime in a way that Mansfield only achieved posthumously. Notwithstanding her commercial and critical success, Elizabeth always considered her cousin to be the greater talent. Certainly posterity agrees. Mansfield's reputation has increased over the years with worldwide scholarship, theses, conferences and seminars, as well as ever more volumes of Mansfield's letters – volumes that amount to many more thousands of words than Mansfield's entire literary output.

The French cottage in Menton, France, where Mansfield lived is preserved in honour of the memory of her brief residence and a blue plaque marks her home in London. In her birthplace of Wellington, a plaque at her old primary school memorialises New Zealand's most famous writer, and the Katherine Mansfield Museum is much visited. There is even Katherine Mansfield merchandise, including gift packs of handkerchiefs accompanied by quotations from Mansfield stories. In contrast, the only existing memorial to Elizabeth is a statue in Buk, Poland, close to the original site of Nassenheide, erected in 2015.

Why one writer has flourished and the other has disappeared from cultural memory isn't altogether explained by unequal talents, even if that were the case. Perhaps an impoverished short story writer who dies at thirty-two of tuberculosis is far more appealing to a literary audience than a wealthy, healthy novelist. Mansfield's modernist dark stories also appeal to the literary fashion that remains with us to this day: a literature of despair and dystopia, of cynicism and that perennial favourite – irony.

Although Elizabeth was a supremely gifted satirist, she was also what David Foster Wallace might have categorised as 'sincere' in her approach. Towards the end of his life, Foster Wallace, one of the most significant writers of the twentieth century, expressed his deep reservations about the all-pervading, possibly pernicious influence of irony in contemporary culture. Despite being a virtuosic ironist himself, he argued that 'the next real literary "rebels" might well emerge as some weird bunch of anti-rebels', predicting that they would retreat from irony and 'have the childish gall actually to endorse single-entendre principles'.

What Foster Wallace was daring to suggest was that there are limits to irony. While irony may be 'a creative rejection of bogus values', and has worked extremely efficiently for rejecting and exposing false values, it cannot create anything with which to replace those values. So we are left in a post-ironic void.

The great achievement of Elizabeth's writing was her ability to combine both irony and satire with a sincere faith in beauty and goodness. And it's perhaps this faith that most distinguishes her from her now more revered and recognised cousin, Katherine Mansfield. But it's also this faith which makes her deeply unfashionable.

One of the many biographers of Katherine Mansfield, Antony Alpers, described the fundamental difference between Mansfield and Elizabeth as due to the 'gulf that separates the religious from the non-religious temperament'. Faith, or a religious sensibility, often implies a conservative closed-mindedness but this was not so for Elizabeth. In fact, one commentator believed the difference between the two cousins could be defined as the difference between the conservative and the radical, with Elizabeth holding the radical position.

'Nobody knew what passed in Katherine's mind,' Frank Swinnerton remarked.

> It was egocentric; and it had two chief preoccupations, Art and her own unmatured childishness. She never grew up. She pretended a great deal to herself, especially about Art [but] she was prevented by ineradicable conventionality from being whole-heartedly bohemian.

On the other hand, according to Swinnerton:

> Elizabeth's mind did mature ... She wept real tears; her sentimentality found release in cruelty and the bold exploration of young men's natures; but she was not, I think conventional. Nothing, as far as I could tell, shocked her.

'Ineradicably conventional' is not a phrase often applied to Mansfield and not many people would describe Elizabeth – with her taste for titles and furs – as bohemian, and yet there is something in this observation from a man who knew them both personally that is convincing. Elizabeth's profound sensual enjoyment of all things earthly is in stark opposition to Katherine's asceticism. Mansfield notes in her journal after a visit from her cousin:'Elizabeth came wearing her woolly lamb. A strange fate overtakes me with her. We seem to be always talking of physical subjects. They bore and disgust me ...'

Where Mansfield rejected the physical world, Elizabeth embraced and rejoiced in it. She was born, as her sister noted, with a temperament 'formed of joy and mirth' whereas Katherine, according to Liebet, had 'a distrust of happiness [that] seems to have come naturally and early'. This sort of distrustful temperament sat comfortably with Modernism and also, it might be argued, with the cynical, sophisticated view held by the educated of our contemporary world. But it stands in stark contrast to Elizabeth's faith and ability for rapture.

In a 1920 letter to John Middleton Murry, Mansfield wrote that her cousin's faith in her own vision was so assured that 'she wants no other'. She went on to say:

I sometimes wonder whether the act of surrender is not the greatest of all – the highest ... Can it be accomplished or even apprehended except by the aristocrats of this world? You see it's so immensely complicated. It needs real humility and at the same time an absolute belief in one's own essential freedom. It is an act of faith. At the last moments like all great acts it is pure risk.

Perhaps only someone as confident in her faith as Elizabeth could have the courage and the fearlessness to indulge in such pure risk. And maybe this letter from Katherine is a recognition of her own comparative lack of courage. Irony and cynicism, after all, feel so much safer. In another letter from Mansfield she seems to be pleading with her cousin to reveal the secret of her lighthearted and joyous approach:

> Dear Elizabeth, I have not thanked you even for *The Enchanted April*. It is a delectable book; the only other person who could have written it is Mozart ... How do you write like that? How? How?

The comparison is an insightful one. Mozart, particularly in his early compositions, also displayed a light, bright simplicity and those who love Mozart will probably love Elizabeth in the same way, for the same reasons – because they are bringers of beauty and pure, sunny delight. And if she didn't always please the reviewers, she certainly pleased her readers. Mansfield signed off the letter:

> Goodbye my dearest cousin. I shall never know anyone like you. I shall remember every little thing about you for ever.

> Lovingly yours, Katherine.

It was the last letter that Mansfield ever posted.

In 1924 Elizabeth tried to visit Katherine Mansfield's grave but was unable to locate it at Fontainebleau. It turned out that John Middleton Murry had been so busy posthumously publishing his deceased wife's work that he had forgotten to pay the maintenance fee for her final resting place. This oversight had resulted in her body being moved to a communal grave. Elizabeth immediately made the necessary payments and arranged for a gravestone; it is only thanks to her devotion to her cousin that the literary pilgrims of today can pay homage to the memory of Katherine Mansfield.

Only months after her separation from Francis, Elizabeth attended a party given by the writer Arnold Bennett where she met the young, good-looking, highly intelligent and impoverished Cambridge undergraduate Alexander Stuart Frere-Reeves. She was fifty-four. He was twenty-four. There appears to have been an instant attraction.

An ambitious young man just starting out in publishing, Frere-Reeves was clearly bewitched by literary celebrity, while Elizabeth, as always, was charmed by handsome youth. (Swinnerton once described her as 'an aging flirt'.) By the end of the party, Elizabeth had invited Frere-Reeves to the chalet for the summer on the pretext of employing him to catalogue the books in her library even though, according to her daughter, she 'had never shown the least desire to have them systematically arranged'. It was to be the beginning of a love affair that would last almost twelve years.

Frere-Reeves was the 'love-child' of an acquaintance of Elizabeth's, Mary Frere, and a Colonel Reeves. The unwanted child had been placed in an orphanage where he remained ignored by both parents until adulthood. As well as being attractive to Elizabeth, Frere-Reeves may well have been someone she felt was a worthy object of sympathy and rescue.

Other guests at the chalet in the summer of 1920 included Bertrand Russell, poet and translator Robert Trevelyan, Augustine Birrell, biographer of Charlotte Brontë, and literary critic William Hazlitt. Frere-Reeves clearly would have felt the privilege of being in such august company and appears to have taken his role of employee seriously, assuming as many tasks as possible, and becoming, in essence, a full-time secretary to the authoress. Among the other guests, he and Elizabeth became known as Little E and Little Oui, because the young man was such a devoted, dog-like yes-man, willing to carry out her every command in order that his employer could devote herself to writing.

Notwithstanding her duties as a hostess to her constant stream of guests – all of whom arrived expecting to be fed and entertained, often for weeks at a time – Elizabeth always maintained a strict writing schedule. She worked in the morning until lunch, took a break, which usually involved a walk, and then worked again until tea, and then again until eight. Her method involved a series of little hard-backed exercise books in which she composed the first draft of a novel in her loose handwriting. She then typed her draft, using two fingers and triple spacing, onto foolscap paper. After making her corrections she typed it out again and corrected again. The final draft was then sent to her publisher and published, apparently, almost exactly as submitted, with little or no editorial interference, although one biographer claims that regarding female sexuality 'she had been inhibited by her publishers about what she could mention'. Perhaps the nearest she ever came to writing a sex scene were a few lines in *Fräulein Schmidt and Mr Anstruther*: 'Some of those words you rained down on me on Tuesday night between all those kisses came throbbing through my head, throbbing with great throbs through my whole body ...'

What, I can't help wondering, might have been censored from this scene and many others in Elizabeth's novels?

By the beginning of 1921 Elizabeth was again the recipient of a series of love letters, this time from the besotted Frere-Reeves:

I find myself pinned down by dreams, dreams of the unattainable. Yet – 'thou art so true that thoughts of thee suffice to make dreams true and fables histories'. Aren't you glad to be idealised – even by such an insignificant being as myself?

The letters got increasingly needy as he imagined Elizabeth companionless at the chalet.

Sometimes I try to imagine your day, try and think what it's like with the terrace under snow – whether everything is different – what you look at when you have breakfast out on the porch … Are you still alone? All your evenings I see you sitting in the corner by the stairs to a little meal and then on a big sofa in front of a bigger log fire.

He asked for a copy of the photo of Elizabeth that had appeared in *Tatler* and told her that, 'Nobody writes to me except you so you can guess how eagerly I look forward to a letter from you.'

By this stage Elizabeth was having second thoughts about yet another romantic relationship. Perhaps she had enjoyed a dalliance but didn't really want the intense neediness of a young man's overwhelming desires. She had been seduced once before by passionate love letters and maybe the danger of leaping into another liaison so soon after Francis was dawning on her. Possibly as a way to avoid making a decision, Elizabeth embarked on a voyage to Italy, a trip that led her to an ancient castle by the sea in Portofino, the setting of, and inspiration for, her most popular novel of all, *The Enchanted April*.

This book, written in a mere three months, and directly after the 'macabre' *Vera*, is a hymn to happiness and a testament to Elizabeth's commitment to recovery and also to her optimistic nature. In the introduction to the New York Review Books edition, Cathleen Schine describes it thus: 'It's a novel about beauty, and it is beautiful; it is about the senses, and it is sensual; but, most important, it is a novel about happiness that makes one happy.'

The novel opens with four women in rain-sodden, post-war London wishing for escape: two unhappily married, one a lonely widow and the fourth, the exquisitely beautiful but much harassed, Lady Caroline.

The somewhat implausible premise of *The Enchanted April* is a promise of spiritual transformation as a direct result of weather, landscape and architecture – in other words, simply by being in an environment of beauty. The women take up residence in the medieval Castello San Salvatore and under the spell of the enchanted surroundings, all the characters magically transform from various states of frustration and unhappiness to moods of contentment and love. The simplest of things – sunlight, flowers, rest – bring about their transformations, and the story becomes a kind of spiritual make-over show.

The two married women, the uptight Mrs Arbuthnot and the possibly mentally unstable Mrs Wilkins, blossom in different ways. At first, Mrs Arbuthnot is slow to allow herself to indulge in joy; as a priggish slave to her local church she has spent her life devoted to good works and is suspicious of enjoyment that doesn't have a utilitarian social improvement attached, 'convinced that morality is the basis of happiness'. She is wracked, for example, by scruples about the extravagant cost of the holiday rental in Italy and how many shoes the money might have provided the poor children in her parish: 'Sixty pounds for a single month ... Before Mrs Arbuthnot's eyes rose up boots: endless vistas, all the stout boots that sixty pounds would buy.'

Unlike her companion, Mrs Wilkins has no sense of guilt about her holiday. She is a kind of mystic who believes, almost religiously, in the possibility of – even the right to – happiness. Perhaps because of this belief, she is the first of the four to transform, rising to a state of rapture soon after arriving at the castle. Within days she turns to her friend:

'Were you ever, ever in your life so happy?' . . .

'No,' said Mrs. Arbuthnot. Nor had she been; not ever; not even in her first love-days with Frederick. Because always pain had been close at hand in that other happiness, ready to torture with doubts, to torture even with the very excess of her love; while this was the simple happiness of complete harmony with her surroundings, the happiness that asks for nothing, that just accepts, just breathes, just is.

By the second day at San Salvatore both women have reached a state of serenity and 'their happiness was complete. Their husbands would not have known them . . . they were just cups of acceptance.'

Lady Caroline, the younger and as yet unmarried beauty, takes a little longer to transform. She is seeking an escape of a specific kind: as a woman of involuntary seductive powers, she wants to be free of unrelenting sexual harassment. She therefore despairs when male visitors arrive at San Salvatore because all men, in her experience, are 'grabbers'. 'Oh no, not another man,' she reflects. 'Looks like a grabber. Grab, grab, grab ...'

> That look, that leaping look, meant that she was going to be grabbed at. Some of those who had it were more humble than others ... but they all, according to their several ability, grabbed ... Sometimes it was just as if she didn't belong to herself, wasn't her own at all, but regarded as a universal thing ...

This theme of unwanted male attention runs throughout the novel as well as the beautiful 1992 cinematic interpretation featuring Joan Plowright and Miranda Richardson that was produced, ironically, by the now-famous sexual harasser Harvey Weinstein. Despite Lady Caroline's fears of a masculine presence ruining her refuge, she also finds peace at San Salvatore. Within days she becomes 'permeated beyond altering by the atmosphere, she no longer thought of it or noticed it; she took it for granted. If one may say so ... she had found her celestial legs.'

Mrs Fisher, the widow in her sixties, being older and more ingrained in her habits of grumpiness, isn't so easily transformed. On first arriving at the castle she is completely devoted to the 'Great Men' of the past – her departed husband, her deceased father (a distinguished literary critic), and the famous dead poets – Byron, Tennyson and Browning. She is also completely dependent on her walking stick. Mrs Fisher's mission in life is to maintain the standards – literary and social – that she feels have begun to slip since the turn of the century. She is firmly of the opinion that women left on their own will naturally fall into promiscuity and, as the elder, considers it as her responsibility to rein in her companions when they start speaking freely about their husbands.

'In my day husbands were taken seriously,' she announces sternly as the four women gather around the dinner table, 'as the only real obstacle to sin.'

She is further alarmed by an exclamation by her companion Mrs Wilkins, who offers a defence of the frivolous chat among friends:

'Why, we've got positively nothing to do here, either of us, except just be happy. You wouldn't believe,' she said, turning her head and speaking straight to Mrs Fisher … 'how terribly good Rose and I have been for years without stopping, and how much now we need a perfect rest.'

The upright Mrs Fisher is immediately struck by the certainty that being happy is anathema to being good and is afraid such an attitude will inevitably undermine morality during their stay at the castle. As she leaves the room without a word, she makes a commitment to herself with regard to the wayward Mrs Wilkins: 'She must, she shall be curbed.'

In the end, even this sour matriarch is not impervious to the magical atmosphere and comes to experience, almost against her will, a youthful sprouting akin to green leaves unfolding from within. The other women notice the change in Mrs Fisher and when the talk turns to the subject of secrets, they playfully tease their elder companion about being so righteous that she couldn't possibly have anything to hide.

> 'Oh haven't I!' exclaimed Mrs. Fisher, thinking of those green leaves ... What Mrs. Fisher was thinking was how much surprised they would be if she told them of her very odd and exciting sensation of going to come out all over buds.

Elizabeth's wording is unusual here but I understand her to mean that Mrs Fisher's spiritual transformation manifested in a feeling of coming into flower, a kind of blossoming of an internal garden.

By the time the quartet of women depart from San Salvatore, the walking stick that Mrs Fisher had previously believed indispensable to her everyday existence – her missing piece – is left behind. While at the castle she has been miraculously raised from a state of dourness that was crippling her both physically and spiritually to a woman once more warmly connected with her living companions and her own inner glow. She has been, in essence, resurrected from spiritual death.

The last page of the novel reflects on the final sunlit days at San Salvatore:

To lie under an acacia tree that last week and look up through the branches at its frail leaves and white flowers quivering against the blue of the sky, while the least movement of the air shook down their scent, was a great happiness.

The picture of great happiness under an acacia tree in bloom on the last page of *The Enchanted April*, I am convinced, was derived from a real-life experience – in Portofino, in Pomerania, in the Swiss mountains and, possibly in harbourside Sydney, where acacia trees, or what we call wattle, would have been in flower for the first three summers of Elizabeth's life.

For a woman who travelled so much, socialised intensely and spent so many of her waking hours at her desk writing books, it is astonishing how often Elizabeth also managed to find time to spend entire days lying in the sun under trees without a hint of guilt about enjoying her idleness.

Happiness Principle Number Eight:
 Leisure

A hundred years after the publication of *The Enchanted April*, the idea that enjoying yourself is unethical – essentially the attitude of Mrs Arbuthnot – is still alive and well today – hence the popular pairing of 'guilty' and 'pleasure'. Contemporary utilitarian philosophers such as Peter Singer, for example, would certainly disapprove of holidays in Italian castles, demanding that we interrogate every purchase and exchange such indulgences for donations to worthy causes. Undoubtedly Singer would have counselled Mrs Arbuthnot to buy the boots for the parish children rather than the ticket to Portofino.

Even art itself is increasingly at the mercy of this kind of thinking – almost as though the value of a painting or a novel or a symphony could be reckoned on the basis of its measurement in relation to social improvement or moral good. 'We're talking less about whether a work is good art but simply whether it's *good*,' commented a 2018 *New York Times Magazine* article, ' – good for us, good for the culture, good for the world.'

The reviews of *The Enchanted April* were mixed. Rebecca West described the novel as 'a disaster' (although her relationship with H.G. Wells may well have influenced her professional judgement of her rival's work). Others found it 'slight' and 'airy' and beyond credulity. Despite being reviewed alongside such greats as Steinbeck, Wharton and Rhys, Elizabeth knew she wasn't taken seriously in the world of literary heavyweights of the time, and that her work, as she had noted, was 'playing in isolation'. But as the scholar Alison Hennegan points out, Elizabeth had always been isolated:

an outsider for most of her life: a colonial at the heart of Empire; a British bride in *Junker* Germany, the widow of a German baron remarried into British aristocracy ... an aristocrat (but only by marriage) ... an anti-Nazi in a casually anti-Semitic world.

There were, however, also a number of glowing reviews. *The Observer* wrote that 'the whole book is a radiant mixture of gentle mirth and sarcasm' and concluded that the author 'has never written more freely, gaily, or slyly'.

The Enchanted April is a fairy tale of sorts which has a happy ending for all. But will their transformations withstand the return to the dismal reality of wet London? The novel expresses no concern for, or prediction about, what comes next; it has simply offered the possibility of a brief period of happiness. Elizabeth's argument is that environments of beauty – be they natural, architectural or artistic – are conducive to contentment and to that extent we can help to create the right conditions for happiness.

There is one theory about happiness that asserts that we all have 'a happiness set-point', more or less built in, and that whatever happens to us – winning the lottery or losing a leg – we will always return to that particular pre-set level. Whatever state life throws us into – an ecstatic high because of falling in love, for example, or a low because we're suddenly disabled by illness – we will always gravitate back to our stable set-point. Then there's the counter argument; that although we generally do have a happiness set-point, it is *moveable*. Entire academic tomes have been written about precisely this subject: the stability (or instability) of the happiness set-point. Are we born with an already fixed capacity for happiness or can we increase it?

The latest research results are optimistic and argue that we *can* alter our set-points. But do I really need scientific proof that happiness set-points are adjustable? Elizabeth has already taught me that fact without my ever having to study a single table of quantitative surveys or interpret results of randomised trials. For which I am joyfully grateful.

By the time Elizabeth returned from her travels in June 1921, Frere-Reeves had become desperate.

> Dear Lady Russell,
> I've not heard from you for ages ... My heart has been all numbed up for so long now it has almost forgotten how to be warm ... I wonder if the sunshine will ever come back?

Elizabeth relented and invited her young admirer back to the Chalet Soleil for the summer. Frere-Reeves gradually made himself so indispensable to the running of what had essentially become a guesthouse that he was nicknamed L.G., short for *Leiber Gott*, or 'Little God'. By September, L.G. and his employer were often setting out on mountain walks on their own, during which the young suitor would read aloud from Keats and Wordsworth 'and at some point during that summer they became lovers'.

Despite the thirty-year age difference, Frere-Reeves recognised Elizabeth's uncanny capacity for joy and given that his life, to that point, had consisted of abandonment and loneliness, it is not surprising he became such a devoted lover. As Walker notes in her biography: 'Their age difference meant nothing to him; he had never had this kind of love and neither had she.'

By the time Elizabeth and Frere-Reeves initiated their affair, he had come to think of her as his saviour, and also, perhaps, as the mother he'd never had. According to Elizabeth's daughter, her mother's greatest gift to her young admirer was spiritual. While staying at the chalet 'his mistrust and bitterness fell from him like a garment,' writes Liebet, 'and he stood forth radiant with the happy spirit of the place'. She continues: 'Like so many of his generation, [Frere-Reeves] was given to perpetual gnawing doubt of established values, to a cynical disbelief in goodness and beauty.'

Elizabeth soon realised that her optimism was not enough to cure her young lover of his intense, dark moodiness. The following summer she records Frere-Reeves 'held forth in blistering language on life,' lecturing her with 'awful theories' about how 'only a vast contempt [of the world] made one safe'.

She puts it down to him being unwell, 'and having one of his nerve attacks'. Later she quotes to him: 'He who has learned to disdain has brought security at the price of the flower of happiness.'

Yet when Frere-Reeves left the chalet at the end of the summer of 1922, Elizabeth felt his absence keenly, and wrote to her young lover: 'You can't think how *empty* the chalet is. Just as if there weren't a soul in it ... I loved your letter.' The isolation dampens her mood and her diary entry on her birthday in August reflects her loneliness. 'No letters ... Dreariest birthday for a long time'. Later she wrote to Frere-Reeves: 'I felt quite injured because, having been with me my last two birthdays, you weren't here this one ...'

Because Frere-Reeves worked in publishing, philosophical discussions with Elizabeth about optimism and pessimism were often in a literary context. When Reeves sent Elizabeth a copy of a D.H. Lawrence novel she responded by saying that although she admired Lawrence, she believed 'he is too submerged in that ugly treacle of bad things and people which is only one part of life'.

On receiving a book by Rebecca West, also sent by Frere-Reeves, she confessed her inability 'to wade through the thick black stuff' that constituted West's 'dark scowlings at life'. She reflected on her own work in comparison: 'If her book is too full-blooded, and all the blood in it black, mine is too thin-blooded, and its blood pale pink.' She went on to describe *The Enchanted April* as 'like a thin flute playing all by itself on an empty afternoon'.

Although this sounds like self-deprecation – and to an extent it is – Elizabeth was also contented with her writer's voice. She insisted on continuing to play her flute, however thin, amid the 'thick black stuff' of the literary fashion of the time, highlighting an important aspect of her philosophy. While so many writers, particularly of the Modernist era, focused on the dark side, Elizabeth, against the tide, insisted on keeping an optimistic focus, creating comic novels characterised by hope and mostly, but not always, happy endings. It was a daring and unconventional insistence that few writers, before or since, have had the courage to sustain.

Frere-Reeves and Elizabeth spent the Christmas of 1922 together in a cottage on the Isle of Wight, possibly to stay out of sight of the private detectives that Francis Russell had employed in an effort to prove adultery and therefore procure an official divorce. Christmas Day was peaceful but all was not perfect. The imbalance in the relationship – of age, of social status, of emotional maturity – soon began to show.

In the new year, Frere-Reeves was often 'livery and cross'. Elizabeth refers to him as 'a poor little thing' and blames his moods on illness but the impression is of someone who is mentally unstable and almost certainly over-dependent on his mature lover. Elizabeth noted that 'his moods' were becoming 'tiresome' and yet as soon as they were separated, she wanted him back. This was to become a pattern. Following his next visit to the chalet, Elizabeth became so rattled by Frere-Reeves she refused to see him off at the end of his stay. Once he had gone, however, she immediately felt his absence and wrote:

> I miss you very much … I think a lot of lovely things – you'd be surprised <u>what</u> a lot and <u>how</u> lovely. My thoughts are like bees, busy swarming 'round sweet things. Ever yours. E.R.

And then a few days later:

> Your letters are the greatest joy to me dear L.G. … There's such a lot I want to say to you, and such nice things, you've no idea what nice things I can say if I give my mind to it – and write too. You have told me you think I might be good at invective if I let myself go but I say to you that if I let myself go to the opposite of invective it would astonish you. Goodbye and bless you.

By the end of the month, the memories of Frere-Reeves' recent bad behaviour at the chalet had faded into insignificance:

> It's like a dream, your visit. I felt too melancholy when the dusk engulfed you, and wandered round the empty house like a lost sheep, went into your room … Don't think about differences and arguments – only think of resemblances and all the laughter and happiness.

And it seems that her longing was as much physical as emotional:

> How I babble on and don't say any of the only things I really <u>want</u> to say. But the things I want to say are things of such sheer beauty that the very notepaper would feel embarrassed and as if it were too thin and cheap to bear them. I'll get some vellum and a pen of gold to put them down in splendid lettering.

Psychologists, I suspect, would define Elizabeth's relationship with Frere-Reeves as unhealthy and co-dependent. She patiently suffered his regular black moods and nursed him during his frequent bouts of ill-health – giving him the mothering he'd never had in the hope, no doubt, that she could 'fix' him – and bring him to mental and physical wellness. I assume that the strength of their relationship was sexual compatibility. Although I don't have solid evidence for this theory, her fear of embarrassing her notepaper strongly suggests the specific kind of yearnings she is too discreet to express in words.

My other reason for this theory is based on personal experience. My own relationship with a man twelve years younger than myself began purely out of physical desire while my husband was overseas for two months on a work exchange. I had no intention of allowing the affair to last but once it had started, it seemed impossible to end, no matter how many times I tried. The fall-out for my family was devastating: divorce, the loss of our beautiful home, and serious upheaval for my children.

The relationship, however, endured for ten years largely because we continued to enjoy the deep, consoling pleasure of sex.

On returning to London, Elizabeth was once again courted by admirers as a literary celebrity and her journals record a period of almost unmitigated happiness. But that happiness, her daughter believed, was primarily due to 'the solid security of being, however unsuitable, the very centre, the guiding star in the life of just one'.

Frere-Reeves continued to adore Elizabeth unconditionally with a kind of love that she had longed for all her life. Although she had moments of mistrust for her own feelings towards him, the alternative of being a woman alone in her mid-fifties did not appeal. She was intensely aware of the loneliness of the elderly and found the blind, feverish love of a young man utterly beyond resisting. (This is a folly of which I am also guilty but after years of moral self-flagellation, I have finally forgiven myself. What warm-blooded woman, I wonder, *could* resist a sexy, handsome, much younger man repeatedly offering his undying love?)

For Frere-Reeves, his relationship with Elizabeth was not only loving but useful. She introduced him into a society he would never have had a chance to mix with otherwise, took him to parties and dinners, and arranged a meeting with her American publisher, Frank Nelson Doubleday, which eventually led to a job offer. Later, as the managing editor of Heinemann,

Frere-Reeves would nurture such writers as Graham Greene and Somerset Maugham. For Elizabeth, there were also extra benefits to the relationship. Frere-Reeves introduced her to his friends, which helped her to feel young. Attempting to stay young, an obsession for many a middle-aged woman, would be the theme for her next novel.

When one of my daughter's friends spied me walking down the street with my younger lover, she immediately called my daughter, clearly impressed.

'Ooh!' she cooed. 'Your mum's a cougar!'

And although my daughter's favourite television series was *Sex and the City*, that didn't mean she wanted her own mother to turn into a Samantha. A cougar may be cool but most people don't want to be related to one.

If Elizabeth was carrying on her affair with Frere-Reeves these days, she would also, presumably, be called a cougar. And although she was strong-minded enough to ignore disapproval of her highly unconventional relationship, she was also besieged with doubts, which was why the working title of her next novel was *I Never Should Have Done It*. Did she mean this sincerely or ironically? Whatever her intention, if I ever write a book about my own fateful affair, I intend to plagiarise it.

The long liaison between Elizabeth and Frere-Reeves provided the writer with the material for her next novel, *Love*, published in 1925, while the affair was still in full swing. The story tells of a forty-seven-year-old widow and a twenty-four-year-old man who embark on a relationship which is disapproved of by friends, family and society. Catherine and Christopher meet at a performance of *The Immortal Hour*, a production that they both attend repeatedly. Christopher pursues Catherine who, like Elizabeth, is girlish and full of attractive energy, despite her age. Christopher, like Frere-Reeves, has been motherless from the age of three and is desperately seeking female attention.

In the beginning, Catherine avoids telling Christopher that she has a grown daughter, Virginia, who has recently married Stephen, a clergyman nearly forty years her senior. When Catherine and Christopher's relationship is revealed, the sanctimonious Stephen is so appalled that he forbids any contact between the unconscionable mother and his wife, whose 'condition' – pregnancy – makes her particularly vulnerable to moral corruption. Stephen announces to the nineteen-year-old Virginia:

'It is shameful ... that some one so much older should even think of love in connection with some one so much younger. Do you not see it is terrible to marry some one young enough to be your son?'

Virginia, however, has enough of her mother in her to answer:

'But is it any more terrible than marrying some one young enough to be your daughter?'

And so the elephant in the room – the hypocrisy of the situation – is finally aired, although not resolved.

Upon being rejected by her nearest family, Catherine considers 'turning her back on everybody' and 'giving herself up to forgetting' by settling somewhere 'in Africa or Australia'. Instead, through a comical series of events, Christopher is obliged to marry Catherine in the hope of making the union respectable. And this is when the relationship begins to go awry. Before the wedding, Catherine loves Christopher but not romantically; the novel tells us that her mirror was 'radiant with the cool happiness of not being in love'. But when she agrees to marry him, everything changes.

The honeymoon in the Isle of Wight is far from sweet – like all the honeymoons in Elizabeth's books, as well as in her life. Catherine cannot match Christopher's physical energy and she is overcome with tiredness. Her radiance fades and her mirror begins to reflect an aging, middle-aged woman. As the days pass the young man feels increasingly house-bound, and dreams about doing a round at the local golf links rather than staying indoors reading poetry and rhapsodising. 'Marriage being mainly repetition, and Christopher now being a husband,' says the narrator, 'he presently began to make fewer rapturous speeches.'

After three days, the new husband becomes bored and aches for a break from the strain of having to maintain romantic bliss.

It wasn't possible that he wanted to be away from Catherine yet he did want to, for a few hours, for a little while; why, if only to have the joy of coming back to her ... There had to be interruption, pause, the mind switched off on to something else. How could one ever know the joy of coming back if one didn't first go? ... He couldn't spend another day just sitting about or strolling gently round; he must be up and doing.

But their attempt to rekindle their newly-wedded joy out of doors proves unsuccessful. While walking they meet another couple and Catherine, much to her horror, is mistaken for Christopher's aunt, rather than his wife. 'While the flush faded out of her face', she thought, 'how dreadful it was going to be if every time she was tired people took her for Christopher's aunt.'

So begins the heroine's doomed quest to maintain her fading youth and beauty, in an attempt to keep the adorations of her younger husband. First, she goes regularly to a beautician whose creams, oils, hair dyes and make-up prolong Catherine's desired appearance. But soon this is not enough and she consults a Spanish doctor who offers her a hugely expensive and ineffective beauty therapy administered via X-rays from 'strange machines'. The description of the treatment is very likely to have been based on Elizabeth's own attempts to retain her youthful beauty:

They laid her on a table, and a great machine was lowered to within a hair's breadth of her bare skin, her eyes were bandaged, and crackling things – she couldn't see what, but they sounded like sparks and felt like little bright stabbing knives – were let loose on her for half an hour at a stretch, first on one side of her and then on the other. When this was over she was injected with some mysterious fluid, and then went home completely exhausted.

Love is unlike most of von Arnim's novels because it features a genuine tragedy. Towards the end, Catherine's teenage daughter dies after a long and difficult labour – an event that may possibly echo the grief Elizabeth continued to feel for her own daughter, Felicitas. The loss however, brings with it an important epiphany: Catherine suddenly has an insight into the vanity of pursuing her lost youth and decides to accept her aging self.

When Christopher and Catherine meet amid the tragic post-mortem scene she is without make-up or hair dye and, as a result, her young husband fails to recognise her. Whereas previously she had shrunk from her husband's gaze and always dimmed the lights when he came into a room, now 'Catherine didn't shrink at all, and let Christopher look at her as much as he liked, for she had done with everything now except truth'. Catherine:

… saw for the first time quite plainly; and what she saw in that strange new clearness, that merciless, yet somehow curiously comforting, clearness, was that love has to learn to let go, that love if it is real always does let go, makes no claims, sets free, is content to love without being loved …

On the last page, as the couple are wondering how they will face the future, Catherine deliberately avoids using the word the author chose for the novel's title:

'We'll just—'
    She was going to say, 'love each other very much,' but thought that might sound like making a claim, and stopped.

Underneath the comedy of this novel is an insightful, hard-won examination of various kinds of love – romantic, familial, maternal and religious. The final sentence may well be Elizabeth's final analysis of love, in her book about love, after a lifetime of lovers, but she never felt satisfied with her inconclusive ending. Perhaps the epiphany she finally had was the fact that women – and maybe men too – habitually confuse love and happiness.

My relationship with a much younger man was also roundly disapproved of by my family and for good reasons. I had not only carried on an illicit affair while married to a devoted husband – with all the lying and scheming that such a commitment involves – I had done it with a man who was moody, controlling and given to explosive anger. When I later explained his behaviour to my psychologist she diagnosed a personality disorder. It was much simpler than that. I had fallen in love with an alcoholic.

Growing up in a family of teetotallers, I had never witnessed heavy drinking. At thirteen, I had got drunk with a friend on Brandivino – because that was the fashion in the Shire in the 1970s – and afterwards felt so ill that I didn't go near alcohol again until my mid-twenties. Even then I would sit on one beer for an entire evening.

Over the years of our relationship, my younger lover began his weekly binge-drinking at four o'clock every Saturday afternoon. Week after week, month after month, year after year, every Saturday night I watched him transform from a happy drunk to an abusive tyrant – the kind of Jekyll and Hyde transformation familiar to every partner of an alcoholic. But I didn't realise this was alcoholism because I thought alcoholics were people who drank metho and slept in the gutters. And being a woman, I thought I could save him. Besides, apart from the killer hangover every Sunday morning, the rest of the week brought precious moments of domestic happiness – his habit of bringing me a cup of tea in the morning before he left for work, our routine of practising yoga together every evening, and our shared passion for gardening, in particular orchids, which led to many beautiful late afternoons together in the backyard, as well as moments of excitement each spring as our cymbidiums came into flower and our native orchids unfolded their exquisite blooms.

When I ask myself now why I stayed for so long with an abusive alcoholic the answer is simple: because we had moments – occasionally entire days – of genuine happiness.

𝟤

The release of *Love* in 1925, led reviewers to exclaim that each Elizabeth novel was more radical than the last. *The Guardian* described the writer as 'the most charming *enfant terrible* of modern fiction. Her indiscretions are so continuous, so enormous, that we fear she has given away her whole sex and may have deterred countless readers from the dangers of marriage'. *The Daily News* remarked that *Love* was a 'moving and recurrently amusing book by one of the most brilliant women of genius now living'. Much later, an obituary writer concluded that Elizabeth's novels encapsulated 'the whole of life – certainly in fiction', which is constituted of 'two things: love and consequences'.

Of all her books, *Love* is the novel that Elizabeth struggled with most, claiming she tore up six pages for every one she wrote. Given the novel runs to 120,000 words, it is difficult to comprehend the intensity of her heroic work ethic or even how she managed to fit in anything else around her exhausting writing schedule.

> ... the failure, the blind groping, the constant being lured off the track by attractive and amusing sentences

which dislocate the whole thing, and have, though mourned, to be got rid of ... writing isn't an easy job, and the easier it looks when it is finished the more soul-sweat has really gone into it. But I wouldn't be without it for anything – to be happy one must create.

Happiness Principle Number Nine:
 Creativity

Around 1923 Elizabeth appears to suffer a mysterious illness, perhaps a genuine clinical depression, or what one biography describes as a 'debilitating tiredness', something very similar to the condition suffered by Catherine in *Love* while on her honeymoon. It is likely that, also like Catherine, Elizabeth's depressed state was mostly about the loss of her famously youthful looks. She had often been mistaken as the sister, rather than the mother, of her four daughters and a face-lift at the age of fifty, secretly undertaken in New York in 1917, had further postponed aging. But now there was little left she could do to ward off the inevitable. Added to that worry was the fact that she was deeply divided in herself about the relationship with Frere-Reeves – acutely aware it couldn't last and yet unable to let it go.

Months before I made the decision to run away with my young lover to the south of France – an episode that still evokes feelings of shame as well as memories of pure joy – I had been standing at the kitchen sink one afternoon washing dishes listening to talk-back radio. The conversation was about why so many married women had lost interest in sex. Callers were suggesting various reasons: tiredness, work stress, responsibilities of young children.

I resisted the urge to phone in with a comment that seemed screamingly obvious: 'Women haven't lost interest in sex,' I wanted to say, 'they've just lost interest in sex with their husbands!' It seemed astonishing to me that nobody even countenanced the idea that middle-aged women might be suffering the same sort of sexual yearnings for a younger man as middle-aged men so often do for younger women.

For many women, I've since discovered, it's not until we hit our forties – when we've finally re-established a normal sleep pattern and the kids can get their own Weet-Bix in the morning – that desire resurfaces. A decade of drudgery and then suddenly you wake up. Hey, something's missing! And it's not just the throbbing, as Elizabeth described it. It's sensuality and tenderness and mostly, in my experience, desire.

It seems so unfair that a woman has to wait until she's dried up and wrinkled to experience her sexuality as fresh and clear, when it's all too late! This was the reason why, as a peri-menopausal woman, like Catherine in *Love*, I ended up poring over cosmetics counters and agreeing to have my skin patted and stroked at great expense, even though I had always felt that this public display of physical intimacy on the ground floor of a busy department store was somewhat indiscreet. And also why, eventually, I found myself completely seduced by the promise of restored youth and agreed to a series of appointments with a beautician in the privacy of the Clarins Beauty Room.

My first time filled me with apprehension; even more so when my beauty consultant asked me to undress down to my underpants. As I lay on the table, being creamed and smoothed and de-wrinkled by a complete stranger, I wasn't sure if I felt ravished or relaxed or, in some way, deeply humiliated, even sinful. Afterwards, when I paid for the service I felt distinctly like someone leaving a den of sensuality. Perhaps, for middle-aged women, the nearest thing we have to the red-light district is a secluded beauty parlour playing mood music and lit by scented candles.

At the end of 1923, Elizabeth was advised by her doctor to go on a long and seemingly pointless journey to South Africa to recover her ailing health.

No diagnosis of Elizabeth's illness is recorded and the impression from her journals, as she embarks on her joyless journey to a strange continent, is of someone who is simply running away from herself. All her life, like her father, Henry, Elizabeth suffered from an incurable restlessness, travelling constantly. On this particular trip, which was long and fruitless, she finally seems to have had an insight into this relentless running away: 'Oh how persistently one thinks it must be wonderful somewhere else, and how equally persistently it isn't!'

By the end of 1924, this insight had been forgotten and Elizabeth was planning yet another change of location. The busy-ness of London was becoming exhausting and she decided she needed to return to a pastoral setting where she could again take up gardening. To that end, she bought land in Virginia Water in Surrey, where she had caravanned so many years before. There she built yet another house named White Gates, close to a golf course, which was presumably for the convenience of Frere-Reeves, a passionate golfer.

At this stage in her life Elizabeth was the devoted owner of four dogs, all of whom required long daily walks. She was also supervising the construction of her new home, designing expansive gardens, maintaining a lover thirty years her junior, and writing yet another comic novel, *Introduction to Sally*, about the folly of youth and beauty. No wonder she was tired.

Christmas Eve of 1925 was supposed to be moving-in day at White Gates. Elizabeth had bought a new car, a Morris Bullnose Coupé, which Frere-Reeves drove to Virginia Water. Was the house, the car and the golf course all simply a way of trying to keep the young man in her life? Were these indulgences all an effort to buttress herself against loneliness? On New Year's Day she recorded in her diary:

An offensive
Is expensive.

On her sixtieth birthday Elizabeth received no birthday greeting from Frere-Reeves and immediately knew that his thoughts were elsewhere, probably with another woman. Yet the relationship dragged on half-heartedly for another two years until, during a visit to White Gates, he announced his plans to marry. Elizabeth noted in her diary:

> After lunch he told me things which were distressing to me, and the bottom was knocked out of life. No good pretending it isn't. The rest of the afternoon and evening knife-like in their cutting pain. We walked drearily in the woods … alas, that he couldn't have waited another 2–3 years.

On the same day, Elizabeth received a telegram from her agent Curtis Brown to say that a magazine in the United States had accepted *Love* for serialisation. 'So happy I would have been another time,' she writes. 'As it is I only want to die.'

Did she want to die because she loved Frere-Reeves so much? Or was it purely her fear of being alone? In the weeks that followed, Elizabeth's daughter observed that her mother 'was often too ill to go out, see her friends or work'; symptoms that would be consistent with a deep depression. By December of that year the author was reflecting on something her first husband had said as he lay dying: 'Dollie Dear, if only this stupid life were ended – it's nothing but torture and irritation.'

'And I didn't believe him,' Elizabeth wrote in her diary. 'Now I know.'

It would be another five years before she accepted that the relationship with Frere-Reeves was really over. She did so, however, with a measure of good grace and the two managed to maintain a lasting friendship, as well as genuine affection. Frere-Reeves named his only daughter after Elizabeth, and she also became the child's godmother.

When the couple met up again in 1931, Frere-Reeves recalled her as extremely thin, her face powdered white and scarred by lifting. 'Nevertheless,' he recorded, 'she was still beautiful.'

Another aspect of Elizabeth I find admirable is her ability to remain friends with ex-lovers. She even managed to be civil with the tyrannical and vengeful Francis Russell. I am not on speaking terms with any of my exes and this seems to indicate a childish immaturity, if not a serious character flaw. Although recently I had an experience which may suggest there is hope for change.

I was walking down a street I usually avoid, the street that my ex-lover – (now not so young) – lives in. As part of my avoidance I chose the footpath furthest from his property while fixing my gaze on my feet. When I looked up for a moment, I saw he was standing at his back fence, peering towards me. Our last exchange, two years earlier, had been bitter and through lawyers. On meeting my gaze, he reached down and held up a pot plant. I immediately recognised it was a dendrobium, our favourite kind of native orchid.

'No flowers?' I asked.

'Not yet,' he said with a tone of such hope and expectation that I was flooded, momentarily, with warmth and love.

And then I walked on.

Elizabeth continued her writing discipline, producing *Expiation*, a long novel about adultery, in 1929, and *Father*, about a young woman escaping her oppressive father, in 1931. But the satisfactions of professional success failed to outweigh her sense of impending isolation.

'Extreme loneliness. Too awful being entirely alone and getting old alone. I don't know anybody so alone.' This was the melancholy mood into which Elizabeth had sunk by late 1931. Such self-pity is atypical and she soon turned to her usual cure for gloom – a dramatic change of scenery combined with a construction project.

This time Elizabeth set her sights on the south of France, and a village named Mougins, since made famous by various famous residents, including Picasso. At that time, several of Elizabeth's old friends and liaisons, including H.G. Wells, had also settled in the picturesque village so there would be a ready-made social life. The new house was to be called Mas de Roses and again Elizabeth would design and foster a magnificent garden where she was soon enjoying wallflowers, cannas, irises, roses, mimosa, daisies and stocks as well as ripening fruit from her orange trees. Her depression lifted and her capacity for joy returned.

At this stage of her life, her daughter Liebet believed her mother was coming to realise the 'satisfactions of a woman's later years' and 'there were moments now when she was inclined to value them far beyond the obvious delights of youth'. In a letter to Liebet, Elizabeth wrote: 'Really my happiness is almost frightening ... how happy I am now that I have final cleared so-called loves out of my life!'

The retreat to the French countryside did not remain undisturbed however, as Elizabeth was becoming increasingly aware of the possibility of war. 'Meanwhile Hitlerism rages in Germany,' she wrote to Liebet.

Those Germans continue to be the danger spot of Europe ... They never learn. They are just as pure *Junker* as before the war. They'll drag us all to hell and themselves too – so meanwhile let us *cultivar notre jardin* and love all the heavenly natural joys that are still ours ... I am very happy inside ... inside is a little temple of quiet in which I sit and bless God for so many lovely things ...

Once again, Elizabeth sets an example I wish to emulate. In a time of plague, as in a time of war, I am powerless over most things except the cultivation of my own *jardin*, interior and exterior. Perhaps the most helpful contribution I can make to our troubled times is to create a little temple of quiet.

During this period Elizabeth worked on her only book of non-fiction. She had been encouraged by Frere-Reeves to write a memoir but instead she decided to write her 'dog book', made up of individual biographies of the fourteen dogs she had owned and loved throughout her life. *All the Dogs of My Life* is a kind of unreliable autobiography, weaving delightful recollections of her life with the often hilarious anecdotes about her much-loved canine companions. The book opens with a declaration about why, late in life, she has come to prefer the love of dogs to the love of men:

> I would like, to begin with, to say that though parents, husbands, children, lovers and friends are all very well, they are not dogs. In my day and turn having been each of the above, – except that instead of husbands I was wives, – I know what I am talking about, and am well acquainted with the ups and downs, the daily ups and downs, the sometimes almost hourly ones in the thin-skinned, which seem inevitably to accompany human loves.
>
> Dogs are free from these fluctuations. Once they love, they love steadily, unchangingly, till their last breath.

That is how I like to be loved.
Therefore I will write of dogs.

In 1936, Elizabeth's seventieth birthday was spent in the Provencal countryside, where she recorded in her diary: 'Am definitely an old woman, and I must bear it in mind. One is so much used to being young that one goes on taking it for granted. I must remember, and my looking-glass helps.'

Her next and final work, *Mr Skeffington*, began with a working title of *Birthday Party* and the subject again was aging. Fanny, the once-beautiful heroine is turning fifty and reluctantly coming to terms with her lost looks. She has spent her entire life seducing men and enjoying their attention, marrying only once and briefly. Throughout the novel, she re-encounters the men whose hearts she broke – men who no longer hold any appeal and who have also ceased to find her attractive. 'Beauty, beauty. What was the good of beauty once it was over?' she asks herself. 'It left nothing behind but acid regrets, and no heart at all to start afresh.'

Early in the novel Fanny observes old ladies and imagines her own future:

This other old lady, this one sitting laying her cards, her mouth all pursed up, was real, and in twenty years' time, or perhaps even sooner at the rate she was decomposing, Fanny's mouth might very well be all pursed up too, into a kind of cross little bag. The indignities of age!

Later, the heroine reflects on her vain involvement with younger men.

She had been made a fool of. She had been dragged in the most humiliating of all dusts, the dust reserved for older women who let themselves be approached, on amorous lines, by boys. Why she hadn't even had the excuse some unfortunate middle-aged women have of being rent asunder by unseemly longings. It had all been pure vanity, all just a wish, in these waning days of hers, still to feel power, still to have the assurance of her beauty and its effects.

Scholar Isobel Maddison calls Elizabeth's final novel the writer's 'unwitting final life lesson for women'. Upon reading *Mr Skeffington*, I certainly learnt a life lesson I might have preferred not to – being forced to admit that I too was one of those 'unfortunate middle-aged women' who had been 'rent asunder by unseemly longings' just so I could run away to the south of France and make love in a field of sunflowers with a handsome younger man. Unseemly longings had been my downfall.

Mr Skeffington took longer to write than any other book – an entire three years. She struggled with the ending, as she so often had with her novels, and resolved Fanny's predicament by reuniting the heroine with her long-estranged husband. But the only reason Fanny allows him back into her life is because he has been blinded in the war. Only in this way can she feel at ease – because her husband remains locked in the past, imagining what his wife once was, and unable to see what she has become. The novel was released in 1940, a few months before the author died. It was an immediate commercial success and later produced as a film starring Bette Davis and Claude Rains in 1944.

During the early period of writing her last novel, Elizabeth spent many evenings alone listening to her wireless. After hearing one report in March 1936, she wrote to her daughter that she was 'horrified' by the 'ravings of Hitler and his lot'. Then she revealed her plans to escape in the event of a German invasion:

> Well, darling, when and if the crash comes you'll be all right (for a time anyhow) in America, and I'll be all right too in a different way, for no German bomb is going to catch me alive ... I have made my simple plans.

She is quite blunt about her arrangements: 'You needn't give me another thought darling, because directly the first bombs start I shall put myself to sleep.'

When Liebet responded to her mother's euthanasia plans with alarm, Elizabeth tried to console her:

> If I were 20 years younger I would see it through, because apart from everything else it will be so *interesting*, and in the long run I'm certain the gangsters will get the worst of it, but it would be absurd to take trouble to

hide or get away or things like that at my age, and I shall stay quiet in my garden till the last possible minute, and then with immense dignity settle down to sleep.

By 1939, however, Elizabeth had realised that living with dignity in Mougins was impossible. She wrote to Liebet:

I'm up to my neck in the military. I've got 8 officers sleeping in the house, 25 soldiers sleeping in the garage, a lorry full of ammunition in my garden and a sentinel with a naked bayonet at my entrance day and night, and a soldier with an anti-aircraft gun crouching behind my rosemary hedge.

Being 'by nature an Escapist', she decided it was time to leave her home and join her daughter in the United States where she had settled with her American husband, before 'beastly men like Hit and Muss' arrived to spoil 'such a lovely, promising world and fill it with blood and misery'.

After some research, Elizabeth decided on her destination – the town of Charleston in South Carolina – because she had heard it had 'a lovely winter climate'. In May of 1939, she sold her car, kissed all but one of her six dogs farewell, and travelled to Cherbourg, where she boarded the *Queen Mary* for New York. On arrival, she was thrilled to be reunited with Liebet and her grandchildren but she later recorded in her diary feeling 'deeply exiled'. Nevertheless, her energy and optimism were not to be thwarted.

Undaunted by being in a completely new land and culture, Elizabeth bought a car, got her American driver's licence and drove to New Hampshire, where she took up residence in the Dublin Inn. As the weather cooled, she took to the road again with a plan to spend the winter in Charleston. There she chose a hotel overlooking the river, the 'Gold Eagle', named by its first owner, the Director of the United States Mint, who authorised the first gold eagle dollars, and a venue known for its celebrity visitors. She settled in with her cocker spaniel, Billie, who slept in his own bed beneath a portrait of George Washington. Elizabeth's publisher, Nelson Doubleday, lived on a plantation nearby – 'no doubt bought with the sweat of his authors' quipped Elizabeth – which provided somewhere for the exile to spend Christmas.

Despite her uprooted life, the aging writer appreciated the 'kind Americans', and even more so when *Mr Skeffington* was chosen as American book of the month in 1940 and then optioned for film rights by Warner Brothers. It was also extremely well received in the United Kingdom where the *Times Literary Supplement* declared, 'This is Elizabeth at her best and only those who have, for so many years, waited impatiently for each new book know how very good that can be'.

The 'kind Americans' were so fascinated with their recently arrived exiled author that *Life* magazine produced a profile in April of 1940, which was the only interview Elizabeth was to give in her life (and in which her place of birth was given as England, with no mention of Australia).

In the new year, when asked by her daughter about her

plans, Elizabeth responded that she was going to stay at the Gold Eagle 'till driven away by agile alligators and snakes'. Not surprisingly however, she was unable to contain her interminable restlessness, and was soon on the road again. This time she chose Summerville in South Carolina, and settled into a cottage adjoining the Halcyon Inn, where she intended to spend the winter of 1940. Her daily routine included letter-writing, garden-visiting and a run on the nearby golf links with Billie.

Like her vain female characters in both *Love* and *Mr Skeffington*, Elizabeth remained extremely conscious of her appearance and early in 1941 she arranged for a course of X-rays 'to get rid of my blemishes'. After her first session with the doctor, she notes in her diary that she 'felt queer afterwards, but daresay this was imagination'. And then on each subsequent X-raying she remarked again about feeling unwell directly after the treatment. It seems highly likely that her attempts to retain her beauty contributed to her ultimate demise.

By mid-January Elizabeth was afraid she had contracted flu. The doctor was called and ordered her to stay in bed, 'but I won't' she recorded in her diary. The following day she 'felt better' but still 'weak and queer'. She contacted Liebet, who drove to Summerville, planning to stay for a few days, and immediately her mother improved, believing she had 'practically recovered'. Liebet, however, picked up the same infection Elizabeth was suffering from and took to bed. The doctor prescribed pills for both of them that, according to Elizabeth, 'made us feel well when we aren't really, underneath'.

Indomitable as ever, for the next week, Elizabeth continued to walk her dog daily amid the cold and windy weather. But on 27 January she recorded that her sore throat had returned. The following morning she went out for her usual walk, braving a strong and icy wind. Then, on 29 January, she wrote her final diary entry: 'Lovely day but raw ... Don't feel well.'

On the first day of February Elizabeth fell into a coma and was taken to the Riverside Infirmary in Charleston where she died on 9 February 1941.

Upon her death, *The Times* published a tribute to Mary Countess Russell:

> Elizabeth, by which she was referred to by her many readers, was ... one of the three finest wits of her day ... Everything that 'Elizabeth' wrote was interpenetrated by her unusually vivid and lovable nature and her pervasive sense of fun.

The Saturday Review of Literature reflected on von Arnim's career, blaming the patronising reviews of her novels on male reviewers who 'managed to persuade themselves that, after all, she wasn't a serious author'. R. Ellis Roberts argued that her literary merit had been undervalued because she was a comic writer and 'lethal to one of the best established institutions in the world of ... letters – masculine vanity'. Hugh Walpole wrote a long obituary for the *Daily Sketch:* 'She leaves, undoubtedly, some of the wittiest novels in the English language,' he opined. 'One or two of her books will remain, I think, as minor classics.'

Elizabeth's death was also considered newsworthy in Australia and Melbourne's *Advocate* reported:

For long the identity of 'Elizabeth,' the authoress of *Elizabeth and her German Garden* and a score of other books, was a subject of speculation. She was Elizabeth Mary, Countess Russell, wife of the second Earl Russell, whose title descended to the present earl, the notorious Bertrand Russell, so remarkably gifted, and, alas, so deplorably astray...Wit, glamour, joyousness, truth (sometimes ugly), incisive satire, laughter, beauty, common sense – all are to be found within the books written by 'the author of *Elizabeth and her German Garden*'.

A belated notice published in *The Age* in September 1941 was sub-titled 'Sources of Happiness':

The death in America early this year of Lady Russell, better known as Elizabeth of the German Garden, is regretted by readers all over the world. Among garden lovers especially she had many warm admirers.

After several paragraphs of glowing reflections on her books, it concludes: 'She will not be forgotten. We shall read again those early, revealing books in which she says the things every garden-loving woman has been saying since Eve.'

The obituarist's sub-title was accurate – Elizabeth's books are indeed sources of happiness – but wrong in his prediction that she would not be forgotten. Her style of conventionally plotted novels, however rebellious, insightful or entertaining, soon went out of literary fashion. As Frank Swinnerton remarked: 'Her talent lay in fun, satirical portraiture, and farcical comedy, qualities which are scorned by "the modern dilemma". Her fame has therefore sunk.'

'The modern dilemma' was integral to Modernism. Modernism dined on dilemmas, and dwelt, as Virginia Woolf said, in the 'dark places of psychology'. Most importantly for von Arnim, Modernism didn't believe in happiness. And this mood has continued into our current era: the appetite for post-apocalyptic despair is so pervasive that we have come to expect it as the new normal. In his book, *Hope Without Optimism*, literary theorist Terry Eagleton makes an insightful comment about contemporary novels:

> When they fail to be suitably downbeat, the effect can be arresting. Such as the case with José Saramago's novel *Blindness* at the conclusion of which a group of men and women have their vision abruptly restored. For a contemporary piece of fiction to end on such a joyfully transformative note is almost as audacious as if *Pride and Prejudice* were to conclude with a massacre of the Bennet sisters.

He goes on to observe, in his typically perspicacious way: 'In the era of modernity, gloom appears a more sophisticated stance than cheerfulness.'

This is perhaps the key to Elizabeth's demise: she was demoted to those of the unsophisticated cheerful. It has become more respectable to be depressed, an attitude that signals virtue, and almost socially irresponsible to be happy – a state that is associated with vacuousness. After all, if you aren't depressed by the mess the world is in – ravaged by fire, flood and plague – you are clearly insensitive or uninformed. Perhaps that is precisely why no one reads her novels anymore, because amid our infatuation with darkness, being cheerful has become not only unsophisticated but morally suspect.

However, if Elizabeth's fame was sunk by Modernism, and her sunny outlook is out of sync with our present era of gloom, perhaps it is time to un-sink her. Perhaps it would be worth the bother dredging her up and having a look around the wreck. Perhaps there is gold to be found.

W hen I first went in search of Elizabeth, I got on a ferry.
Ever since I was a child, I have loved ferries because
getting on a ferry meant we were going on holidays. To this
day, just the sight of an old-fashioned ferry makes me happy.
This time I was getting on a ferry because I thought, for
once, I should do what proper biographers do and begin at
the beginning – where my subject was born. Because so far,
all three biographers had got it wrong. The first biographer,
Elizabeth's daughter, knew that her mother was born in
Australia but wasn't sure where. The second claimed she was
born in New Zealand, presumably because she was from the
same Beauchamp family as her cousin, Katherine Mansfield.
And the third, and most recent, who had followed Elizabeth in
all her peripatetic footsteps throughout Europe, but not her
infant footsteps around Sydney Harbour, also misplaced her
subject's birthplace, describing it as 'overlooking Rose Bay' and

remarking 'that the site of her birth is still known as Clifton Gardens'.

This is the kind of mistake that Elizabeth would have delighted in. Clifton Gardens is in Mosman, seven kilometres from Elizabeth's birthplace in Kirribilli, but a completely comprehensible error. What more seductive idea can there be for a biographer than that of your beloved subject, author of romantic hymns to gardening, having had her very beginnings in a garden?

It is typical of Elizabeth that even this simple fact – her birthplace – is difficult, perhaps impossible, to ascertain. She is a paradox of candour and clandestineness, of frankness and dissimulation, of bold forthright opinions and hidden, unspoken judgements. She was well aware that her highly unconventional life would attract biographers and, in an effort to maintain privacy, she burned the bulk of her notes and diaries in what she referred to as 'the holocaust'. The author whose novels featured women who didn't sentimentalise pregnancy, who were frank about the horrors of childbirth, who rejected the endless, uncontrolled bearing of children, who ran away from unhappy marriages, who had affairs, and then ran away from them too – whose novels, in other words, closely reflected her own life – was also the author who wanted to remain private. This woman who was outrageously outspoken in her books also left much unspoken.

The summer I went searching for Elizabeth's birthplace I got off the ferry at Kirribilli, accompanied by the friend who had introduced me to the author more than a decade earlier.

Together we traipsed around the surrounding streets, turning old maps upside down, searching for the site that had once been the setting for Beulah House, the stately home of Elizabeth's parents, Henry and Louey Beauchamp. The word 'Beulah' was used by John Bunyan in *Pilgrim's Progress*, and later by William Blake in his poetry, to mean mystical place between heaven and earth. Perhaps, in 1866, when Elizabeth was born, Kirribilli was exactly that. In a pseudo-memoir of Elizabeth's mother, Beulah House is described as:

> a wonderfully spacious and altogether charming home set in a large garden. Through tall gums there were splendid views over the harbour to Sydney Cove and well laid-out garden steps went right down to the water's edge ...

I had an old sketch of the stately sandstone house that had once stood on one of the most beautiful headlands of the harbour, with a grand porch supported by Doric-style pillars.

After much effort, my friend and I finally found the location of Elizabeth's last home on Kirribilli Point. But it was not a charming, historical homestead built from beautiful Sydney sandstone with spacious gardens. Crowded onto the block that was previously the site for Beulah was an assortment of houses and apartments vying for water views, twenty or thirty in total, leaving no evidence of the grandeur that once was. Below, the Beulah Street Wharf, presumably also once part of the Beauchamps' waterfront property, is all that

GABRIELLE CAREY

remains for the literary pilgrim looking for something to honour this once hugely celebrated Australian author. Professional literary pilgrims might also note that, just around the next headland, another Australian writer, May Gibbs, is splendidly celebrated with the preservation of her house, a museum and café. She even has a ferry named after her.

I went home that day feeling mightily accomplished. My friend and I had identified the site of Elizabeth's last known whereabouts in Sydney. It was here that the only photo of Elizabeth in Australia was taken. It shows a surly little girl with ringlets in a lace dress and silk waistband, wearing slippers and socks, holding a hoop while standing in first position *plié*. On first seeing it, I got very excited about the leafy background with water in the distance. The trees surrounding her, I thought for a moment, looked like banksias. Could this photo have been taken in the garden at Kirribilli?

But one thing I have learnt as a biographer, or 'biografiend' as James Joyce calls us, is that certainties are rare. I was soon disabused of my wishful notions by learning a few basic facts about nineteenth century photography. The portrait had been taken in a studio against a standard 'nature' backdrop. There was absolutely nothing real or Australian about her surroundings. Mystifying me further was the fact that the little girl looked much older than three. Was this photo really taken in Australia, as her descendant assured me, or was this another biographer's trap?

Three is very young to leave a mother country and yet we also know that in the development of the mind the first three years are crucial. The geography of birthplace matters. My sister left her place of birth, England, when she was four but always retained a deep connection to that country, its landscape and its climate, so much so that she requested that her ashes be scattered in the Cotswolds. My first boyfriend had left Italy when he was two and yet retained his first language and plenty of recognisable Italian characteristics. My own daughter left her country of birth, Mexico, when she was a toddler, but still feels more at home in Mexico City than she does in Australia.

So, it seems at least feasible that the beauty of the special Southern Hemisphere light on the sparkling harbour of Kirribilli Point might have made a lasting impression on the young Mary Annette Beauchamp. And even possible that her Pomeranian refuge, the place that was to become her salvation and the inspiration for her first two books, reminded her vaguely of her earliest years. On first discovering the grounds of Nassenheide, Elizabeth wrote:

Wandering out ... into the bare and desolate garden, I don't know what smell of wet earth or rotting leaves brought back my childhood with a rush and all the happy days I had spent in a garden.

She is probably referring to the part of her childhood spent in Lausanne, Switzerland, where the family settled in a chalet and where she spent mornings being tutored and afternoons playing in the alpine fields. However, the biographies don't refer to any specific garden at Lausanne, only to the surrounding trees and fields full of wildflowers. Could she have been remembering the backyard in Kirribilli? Was her effort to create a garden in Prussia also an effort to recreate the garden of her childhood at Beulah? In one of Elizabeth's lesser known novels, *Introduction to Sally*, there is a brief mention of this Australian home:

> ...his mother sat...by the fire in Almond Tree Cottage, a house which used, before the era of her careful simplicity, so foolishly to be called Beulah.

Why was the name Beulah so foolish? Did the name seem primitive and unsophisticated to the Europeanised grown-up Elizabeth whose early childhood was spent in the then semi-rural Kirribilli? Was an awareness of her Australianness just another one of Elizabeth's deep secrets?

The possible references to Australia throughout Elizabeth's novels are few but tantalising. In *The Pastor's Wife*, for example, there is hint at a dimly remembered past when Ingeborg is contemplating an escape from her oppressive family and stops by a travel agency to look at the images of faraway places:

> She stood staring at the picture, half-remembering, trying hard to remember quite, something beautiful and elusive and remote that once she had known – oh, that once she had known – but that she kept on somehow forgetting.

And there is another poignant moment when the heroine again suddenly feels intensely homesick for a place she once knew:

Space, freedom, quiet ... the shining clouds passing slowly across the blue. She wanted to be alone with these things ... with a longing that was like home-sickness. She remembered somehow that once she used to be with them—long ago, far away ... And there used to be little things when you lay face downwards on the grass, little lovely things that smelt beautiful—wild-strawberry leaves, and a tiny aromatic plant with a white flower like a star that you rubbed between your fingers ... She stood still a moment, frowning, trying to remember more; it wasn't in England ... But even as she puzzled the vision slipped away from her and was lost.

Does this homesickness for 'something beautiful and elusive and remote' indicate a distant shore on the other side of the globe? Could there be a floral clue to her half-remembering of this faraway place somewhere around Sydney Harbour? Should I go back to Kirribilli to search for a tiny aromatic plant with a white, star-shaped flower?

At the end of my fellowship spent investigating the life and work of Elizabeth von Arnim, a year which I now look back on as one of the happiest in my life, I arrived back in Sydney extremely nervous about returning to my old existence, my old job and my old house – the interior having been contaminated by thieves and the exterior decimated by the ongoing reconstruction of the garden wall. Every flower, shrub and rose bush I had tended over the past decade was destroyed. The one surviving clivia that greeted me on my arrival, which had bravely struggled through the cement dust to boast its bright orange flower, was quickly trodden on by the builder's boot. I would have to plant my entire garden all over again.

Within months, however, the wisteria was in flower, the vegetable box re-planted, the marigolds in bloom and two climbing roses decorated the magnificent new garden wall. Not long after, the lockdown was announced and during the weeks of working from home, I took to having lunch outdoors under the frangipani tree. Oftentimes, following my salad and cheese and seeded bread, I stretched out on the picnic blanket, and as the world turned in turmoil, I lay in the dappled sunlight pretending I was Elizabeth von Arnim. And even though I was far from Elizabeth's enchanted places – the Swiss Alps, the bay of Portofino, the south of France – I discovered that my own ordinary, unsophisticated suburban garden could also be a genuine place of enchantment.

Elizabeth von Arnim's
PRINCIPLES OF HAPPINESS

Number One: Freedom

Number Two: Privacy

Number Three: Detachment

Number Four: Nature and Gardens

Number Five: Physical Exercise

Number Six: A Kindred Spirit

Number Seven: Sunlight

Number Eight: Leisure

Number Nine: Creativity

Select works by Elizabeth von Arnim

von Arnim, E 1898 *Elizabeth and her German Garden*, Macmillan
Publishers, London.
——1899, *The Solitary Summer*, Macmillan Publishers, London.
——1900, *The April Baby's Book of Tunes*, Macmillan Publishers,
London.
——1901, *The Benefactress*, Macmillan Publishers, London.
——1904, *The Adventures of Elizabeth in Rugen*, Macmillan
Publishers, London.
——1905, *The Princess Priscilla's Fortnight*, Smith, Elder & Co.,
London.
——1907, *Fräulein Schmidt and Mr Anstruther*, Smith, Elder & Co.,
London
——1909, *The Caravaners*, Smith, Elder & Co., London.
——1914, *The Pastor's Wife*, Smith, Elder & Co., London.
Cholmondeley, A 1917, *Christine*, Macmillan, New York.
von Arnim, E 1919, *Christopher and Columbus*, Macmillan
Publishers, London.
Anonymous, 1920, *In the Mountains*, Macmillan Publishers, London.
von Arnim, E 1921, *Vera*, Macmillan Publishers, London.
——1922, *The Enchanted April*, Macmillan Publishers, London.
——1925, *Love*, Macmillan Publishers, London.
Elizabeth, 1926, *Introduction to Sally*, Macmillan, London.
——1929, *Expiation*, Macmillan Publishers, London.
——1931, *Father*, Macmillan, London.
——1934, *The Jasmine Farm*, Heinemann, London.
von Arnim, E 1936, *All the Dogs of My Life*, Heinemann, London.
——1940, *Mr Skeffington*, Heinemann, London.

Works on Elizabeth von Arnim

de Charms, L 1958, *Elizabeth of the German Garden,* Heinemann, London.

Forster, E.M. 1959, 'Recollections of Nassenheide', *The Listener,* Vol. 61, London.

Hardie, X 1988, Introduction to *Vera,* Virago Modern Classics, London.

Hennegan, A 1999, 'In a class of her Own: Elizabeth von Arnim', *Women Writers of the 1930s,* Joannou, M (ed.), Edinburgh University Press, Edinburgh.

Howard, E.J. 1985, Introduction to *Elizabeth and her German Garden,* Virago Modern Classics, London.

Kellaway, D 1993, Introduction to *The Solitary Summer,* Virago Modern Classics, London.

Maddison, I 2012, 'The curious case of *Christine*: Elizabeth von Arnim's war-time text', *First World War Studies,* 3:2, pp. 183–200, Taylor & Francis, <https://doi.org/10.1080/19475020.2012.728740>.

Maddison, I 2013, *Elizabeth von Arnim: Beyond the German Garden,* Ashgate, Surrey, England.

Schine, C 2007, Introduction to *The Enchanted April,* New York Review Books, New York.

Usborne, K 1986, *'Elizabeth': the author of Elizabeth and her German Garden,* Bodley Head, London.

Walker, J 2013, *Elizabeth of the German Garden – A Literary Journey,* Book Guild Publishing, Brighton, England.

Walker, J 2019, 'Family Life on Kirribilli Point in the 1860s: The enigma of Elizabeth's Birthplace', The International Society Devoted to Scholarship of Elizabeth von Arnim, 27 October,

<https://elizabethvonarnimsociety.org/uncategorized/family-life-on-kirribilli-point-in-the-1860s-the-enigma-of-elizabeths-birthplace>.

Other Sources

Anon. 1940, '"Elizabeth" of German Garden Fame, is the Countess Russell', *Life*, 29 April, pp. 106–7, New York.

Coleman, V 2004–2008, Verna Coleman Papers, unpublished research notes, MLMSS 10399, State Library of New South Wales, Sydney.

Eagleton, T 2015, *Hope without Optimism*, University of Virginia Press, Charlottesville.

Elizabeth Mary Russell, Countess Russell Papers, ER 1–1787, Huntington Library, California.

Jones, K 2010, *Katherine Mansfield: The Story-teller*, Edinburgh University Press, Edinburgh.

King, F 1978, *E.M. Forster and his World*, Thames & Hudson, London.

Lowndes, B 1946, *The Merry Wives of Westminster*, Macmillan, London.

Macmillan Archive, correspondence with Countess MA von Arnim 1898–1936, Vols CLXIV, CLXV, British Library, London.

Mansfield, K 1911, *In a German Pension*, Stephen Swift & Co. Ltd, London.

Murry, J.M. (ed.) 1941, *The Letters of Katherine Mansfield*, Alfred A Knopf, New York.

O'Sullivan V and Scott M (eds) 2008, *The Collected Letters of Katherine Mansfield 1922–1923*, Vol. 5, Oxford Univeristy Press, Oxford.

Roiphe, K 2007, *Uncommon Arrangements: seven portraits of married life in London literary circles 1910–1939*, Dial Press, New York.

Sacks, O 2019, *Everything in its place: First loves and last tales*, Picador, London.

Santayana, G 1953, *My Host the World*, Cresset Press, London.

Sheldon, K.M. and Lucas, R.E. (eds.) 2014, *Stability of Happiness: Theories and evidence on whether happiness can change*, Elsevier Academic Press, San Diego.

St Aubyn E 2006, *Mother's Milk*, Pan MacMillan, London.

Swinnerton, F 1963, *Figures in the foreground – literary reminiscences 1917–1940*, Hutchison, London.

Tomalin C 1987, *Katherine Mansfield: A Secret Life*, Viking, London.

Wells, H.G. 1984, *H.G.Wells in Love: Postscript to an Experiment in Autobiography*, Faber & Faber, London.

Acknowledgements

I am grateful to the Australian National University for the 2019 H.C. Coombs Creative Arts Fellowship, during which I undertook much of the research for this book, and also to my ANU colleagues who encouraged me and took an interest in my subject. I am also grateful to Writers Victoria and the Hazel Rowley Literary Fellowship for the Highly Commended Award.

I am indebted to Maisie Fieschi for her invaluable assistance with the difficult job of structuring the manuscript and to Ursula Dubosarsky, who introduced me to Elizabeth von Arnim all those years ago.

I have been greatly assisted by the three previous biographers: Leslie de Charms, Karen Usborne and Jennifer Walker, as well as the generous cooperation of Ann Hardham, executor of the Elizabeth von Arnim literary estate.

Thanks are due to Jacqueline Blanchard and Breanna Blundell for help with the nitty gritty end of the manuscript, as well as Madonna Duffy and Jane Novak for maintaining faith in the project.

The quotation from Terry Eagleton's *Hope Without Optimism* is reproduced with permission of the Licensor through PLSclear. The quotation from Kathleen Jones's *Katherine Mansfield: The Story-teller* is reproduced with permission. The quotations from Francis King's *E.M. Forster and his world* are reproduced by kind permission of Thames & Hudson Ltd, London. Quotations from Isobel Maddison's 'The Curious Case of *Christine*: Elizabeth von Arnim's war-time text' are reprinted with permission of the publisher Taylor & Francis Group, www.tandfonline.com. Quotations from Isobel Maddison's

Elizabeth von Arnim: Beyond the German Garden are reproduced with permission of the Licensor through PLSclear. Quotations from Katie Roiphe's *Uncommon Arrangements: seven portraits of married life in London literary circles 1910–1939* are reproduced with permission. The quotation from Edward St Aubyn's *Mother's Milk* is reproduced with permission of the Licensor through PLSclear. Quotations from Jennifer Walker's *Elizabeth of the German Garden: A Literary Journey* are published with permission. Quotations from *H.G. Wells in Love: Postscript to an Experiment in Autobiography* are reproduced with permission. The quotations from Verna Coleman's unpublished research notes are reproduced with kind permission from her daughter, Ursula Dubosarsky.

Books to read by Elizabeth von Arnim
• The Pastor's Wife p.16
• The Solitary Summer p. 61

Ingram Content Group UK Ltd.
Milton Keynes UK
UKHW021312020623
422780UK00022B/954

9 780702 262975